The
Happiness
Secret

The Happiness Secret

How to Rediscover Lost Happiness

STEVE WOOD

BALBOA.
PRESS

A DIVISION OF HAY HOUSE

Balboa Press books may be ordered through booksellers or by contacting:

Balboa Press
A Division of Hay House
1663 Liberty Drive
Bloomington, IN 47403
www.balboapress.com.au
1 (877) 407-4847

Printed in the United States of America.

ISBN: 978-1-4525-2593-8 (sc)
ISBN: 978-1-4525-2594-5 (e)

Balboa Press rev. date: 11/10/2014

How to Rediscover Lost Happiness

- Simple Guide to Self Awareness
- Understandable Language
- Do-able at Home Self-assessment
- Dispels the Mysteries of the Gurus
- Changes your Diet of Un-Happiness

Contents

Introduction

So much has already been written on this subject of happiness and how it might be achieved. Yet, while none of these works could be described as harmful, few of them could be said to affect enduring happiness either. And happiness *should* be enduring, not momentary, not here today and gone tomorrow. Many such works recommend practising daily rituals like; reciting positive affirmations or sticking notes with power phrases to your bathroom mirror, where you'll see and read them first thing in the morning, then recite the words, perform the acts, and visualise periodically throughout the day. Yet others promote the practice of group therapy, mass confessions while sitting cross-legged and looking into one another's eyes, listening to evocative music, and reciting loving verses. Some claim these practices work, bringing some sense of happiness, while for others, they present even further challenges. Challenges such as invasion of privacy, self-doubt, and the need for self-discipline, fears present in all of us to some degree. You need to be brave enough and patient enough, and have money and time enough, to participate. And of course, you must remember to do it!

Just as with healthy eating and exercise habits, developing healthy happiness habits surely is a good thing to do, but what golden key unlocks the door to a deeper understanding of the human psyche? What key costs nothing and yet provides an effective and doable solution? What key could become an integral part of your everyday life, like breathing?

Conscious awareness is the one and only key that will open the door to your enduring happiness. And it's proven that developing conscious awareness is a doable achievement and will lead you to Self-realisation. It *requires no effort* yet is the only truly effective and lasting solution, and it is fundamental to a life of peace, inner happiness, and meaningful fulfilment.

We each have our life challenges, events that become our "issues," issues that we must somehow deal with to maintain order in our lives. Yet, despite a generally high level of academic education, we struggle to overcome or even come to terms with our ordinary, everyday events. Events such as domestic disharmony, conflict at work, grief, loss of love, sadness, heartbreak, melancholy, and disappointment, all of which can escalate into heavy, life-debilitating psychological millstones. When we examine them, we find that they're all causes of mental stress and that we express the pain we derive from them outwardly, through our emotions. Now, while we cannot hope to stop our life's ebb and flow, what's most important to living a happier life is ensuring that we have the capacity, the knowledge, and the tools to deal with these matters quickly, whenever they arise—better still, before they arise. So, this key to happiness must truly be a golden one!

Unlocking your human psyche is a process, one in which you'll find yourself confronted with the unexpected, a bit like a house renovator confronted with termite damage hidden in critical parts of structural beams. When those termites are eradicated and the rotten beams replaced with new, stronger ones, your house becomes one in which you can live much more at ease, safely, and peacefully.

Within these pages you will find the tools you'll require for the job of discovering and eradicating the causes of your unhappiness. Along the way you'll also discover one of life's most profound secrets, the secret to uncovering what's already within you, the ultimate state of being, that, which in itself, is all empowering, and facilitates the only enduring solution to your personal inner happiness.

By examining anecdotes from other people's lives, all typical and common human behaviours that will resonate with you and your own life experiences, I illustrate just how easily unhappiness might manifest in you too and reside there unbeknownst to you, determining your everyday thoughts and behaviours, often to the great detriment of your everyday life.

But perhaps the greatest gift to be unwrapped here is the teaching of a simple exercise, one you'll do at home, to self-test your unwanted emotions and reach a deeper understanding of what really makes you happy or unhappy. This simple but profoundly effective self-examination will reveal absolute truth and keep you on your happy track always. Without reaching this deeper understanding of yourself, you're unlikely to ever move forward through life without experiencing recurring bouts of emotional disturbance, recurring unhappiness.

Here you will learn how to end that energy-sapping state of affairs, and to conquer your previously unknown, uncontrolled subconscious mind activity bringing intellectual, conscious awareness into your mental field of view. By replacing old, entrenched, destructive life traits and their resulting debilitating emotional reactions with new conscious choices for calm and contentment, enduring happiness will soon prevail.

You'll soon discover that your therapist, your own inner guide to a life of enduring happiness, is already within you. Both happiness and unhappiness are, in effect, matters of your own making and the manifestation of either condition is entirely in your own hands, even more precisely, entirely in your own head.

But just how can you reach into your head to unravel the mystery? Simply by following this guide and being prepared to reinvent your life paradigm, your personal 'inner map' of your world. Be prepared for the possibility of a whole new life experience, the experience of enduring inner happiness, through living from a deeper, hidden part of your being, your inner Self.

This work is your reference book, your "go to" place whenever you need reminding that your number one priority in life is your enduring inner happiness. Accordingly, the information, concepts, and ideas presented here are offered as inspiring gems of wisdom, intelligence to help you overcome your life's difficulties, your unhappiness and to move forward, to enduring happiness. Once Self-awareness is attained, everything else in your life will rise soundly and unfalteringly from there.

As with learning a new language, however, perhaps being outside of your current understanding and your present life paradigm, some aspects and concepts within this work may at first seem a challenge. But then, when you least expect it, they'll awaken you, reinventing your life sensibilities and your understanding of your Self, of Self-awareness, so that in time, with practise and patience, you will become fluent in another, much wiser 'language', a much calmer, happier way of living.

Those of us living within societies with a perceived comfortable lifestyle, without personal threat or urgent need, can tend to become terrible procrastinators. It can take us an eternity to stop doing things we've done habitually all our lives, even after we've determined that those things no longer serve us. But when we finally take the plunge to set out to acquire new knowledge and positive change, to finally do something about a personal goal that we've hoped to achieve, we want to feel assured that the road we eventually take will in fact lead us directly to the results we desire.

Reader, you may rest assured.

If true and authentic inner happiness is your destination, your journey should begin here, because at last, and in simple language, here is everything you need to know about how to get destructive thoughts and life-restricting emotions out of your head and enduring happiness back where it belongs, in your heart....

and to keep it there.

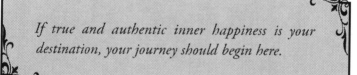

If true and authentic inner happiness is your destination, your journey should begin here.

CHAPTER 1

My Secret Unhappiness

The achievement of happiness, most of us would agree, is the one common goal of all humanity. Seven billion people throughout the world, in hundreds of countries, all with vastly different cultures, lifestyles and opportunities, nevertheless, individually, desire and seek to attain this one thing we call happiness. Happiness has been described variously as an emotional state of being ranging from gladness to ecstasy. And a vast variety of means to achieving it have been offered by the masters of differing beliefs, faiths, and ideologies. "But how," you must be asking, "despite all the wisdom, despite all the wealth in the world and all the reasons you'd expect this state of being to be as natural to us as breathing, does happiness remain so elusive?" Well, my friend, the answer is;

1. We're *unaware* of our subconscious minds.
2. We cannot stop our *thinking*.
3. We *believe* what we think.

Steve Wood

It's a simple enough answer, isn't it? But it has been a very complex issue to untangle, because from our earliest beginnings in life, each of us has had embedded in our subconscious mind unique and complex information giving direction to our individual life journeys. The subconscious is our life-forming crucible and contains the seeds of all that has given rise to the story of our life. From its' archive of all of our experiences, including those of our forebears, our ancestors, has formed, our life paradigm. Although this paradigm *is* the blueprint, for the design and construction of our life, for our values and life choices, it's primarily due to our unyielding attachment to it, that so much *unhappiness* prevails in our life.

When we pause to reflect upon our life journeys, remembering the crossroads and obstacles we encountered, the choices we were offered and directions we chose to take along the way, we might wonder how differently our lives might have turned out had we chosen another, different route. You will relate to this, and of course you may well wonder about it, but you shouldn't fuss about it, because, at the end of the day, you can rest assured that whatever road you *have* taken, it's been the right one. After all, that road has led you to this day, to this moment, and to this book. And at this moment, for better or for worse, your life, and most likely your level of happiness, reflects the sum of all of the choices you've made, the sum of your life's journey to date. What you are about to learn in the reading of this book is also a part of your journey, a part that I hope will enlighten and uplift you, opening up and straightening out your road toward happiness.

So let me begin by asking you this simple question: How *has* your journey turned out so far? Would you describe it as good? Wonderful? Just okay? Wavering, or Miserable? I'm sure that like everyone else on the planet, you will have experienced what you considered both good and bad times, highs and lows. Yes? Whatever the mix, as you take time to read through the chapters ahead, I'd like you to reflect on the bad times, because you see, unbeknownst to you, throughout your life's journey it's actually been the difficulties, the crossroads, and obstacles that you encountered along the way that may have presented you with your greatest opportunities. These were opportunities to make not just subtle changes in direction but profound shifts that would last throughout your whole life. When they presented themselves to you in the past, you may or may not have recognised these as potential life-changing opportunities. That's a matter that you'll be able to determine after finishing this book. For now though, as you set out on this journey of discovery with me, I'd like to begin by telling you about a particular life-changing opportunity that presented itself to me. It happened at about the halfway point in my life journey. Here's how it unfolded.

Perhaps like you, I was born free of unhappiness, born into a financially poor but harmoniously rich family environment, and I grew up in a quiet residential suburb close to the beach. Being the youngest family member, I was always referred to as the baby, a term used by my father when introducing me to his friends. Oh, how I loathed that name as a ten-year-old! Together with my parents, my three older brothers and I lived with my maternal grandmother. We four brothers were well loved and well disciplined by our strict parents, and we were certainly never abused. In our twenties, one by one we left home to marry and pursue our lives and to raise families of our own. Being the "baby," I was the last to leave, and I travelled the farthest in search of a life, a life and lifestyle that would turn out to be vastly different from those of my parents, at least in terms of material matters but, remarkably, very similar in terms of family interconnection and moral and social values.

As I'm sure has been the case for billions of people, as that life unfolded, unhappiness, in its many forms and levels of intensity, became invisibly entangled in my psyche. Its complexities and their embedded effects dwelt there, *unrealised*, for forty-six years. During this period my life challenges were many and varied, yet even the worst events seemed always to be surmountable. I always managed to put even the very tough issues behind me, and to move on. But despite my gritty attitude, unnervingly, too many of them seemed to be repeated over and over again. Too many years were spent living a less-than-happy life, but due to my sense of pride and fear of others learning about my unhappiness, I never talked to anyone about it. My unhappiness was my best-kept secret. Always remaining optimistic that one day all would be well, that better times were ahead and my life would eventually blossom, I put on my happy face. But underneath, somewhere deep inside me, I knew life ought not to be so difficult, so miserable. As I'm certain that anyone suffering unhappiness would agree, my unhappiness was a lonely place.

At the age of forty-six, I'd embarked upon and left behind a number of personal relationships and a variety of careers. I'd rented, bought, or built and sold a score of different homes, lived in several cities in two different countries, and was twice married and twice divorced. Enough said. Yet through all of this, I was lucky enough to have maintained good relations with many friends and my past wives, and I was blessed with two loving children, whose ages' are twenty years apart. Considering myself somewhat finally settled, in both my personal and business life, I established a small but successful real estate business. This brought with it a greater degree of financial stability. I felt prepared now to embark upon a new direction for living, with my new loving partner, Penny. She and I were both ecstatically happy to be together, and especially to be free of our earlier life challenges, including both our disastrous past relationships and all the emotional turmoil attached to them. Life seemed to be on track at last. Thank God! We began building not only a happier new life together, but also a beautiful new home, close to the beach in a peaceful seaside town.

We whimsically named the property Seabird Hill, which was the brand of inexpensive champagne we bought to toast our success on the day we acquired the land. This was to be our dream home, where we'd live out the rest of our lives together. A custom-designed, Old World style home, sitting elevated among the trees on a quiet leafy lane, its living areas were airily spacious, with soaring ceilings, and restfully decorated rooms that opened through French doors to wide, shady verandas. This was the kind of house we'd both dreamed of living in. From kitchen to bedrooms, from bathrooms to basement, it boasted every comfort and modern amenity. We considered it our just reward for hard work and our patience in having endured those former years' many difficulties. This was to be a place where our children and friends would come to stay, to share in our love and happiness. Here, miles from the noise of stressful traffic congestion, crowded shopping centres, and urban confusion, the only sounds to be heard were birdsong and the nearby surf beaches' distant roar and surge over the sand. A rare lifestyle awaited us, one that was a delightful contrast to the life in the city suburbs we so loathed. At last we felt we'd found happiness and a peaceful life in our ultimate environment. Friends told us that we were the envy of many. It was all so perfect. What could possibly go wrong?

Actually ... everything! Burning the house down would not have more disruptive.

You see, the happiness of our refuge soon became unhappiness, due to what seemed to me to be, the past. Not my past, I thought, but that of my new partner. Penny's ex-husband, Ron, had reappeared from oblivion to be constantly in our faces.

To me, he was not a civilised man but an uncouth brute. His intrusion into our lives came initially in the form of rude and abusive telephone calls at all hours of the day and night, both at our workplaces and in our home. Not satisfied with firing volleys of volatility from a distance, he'd personally invade our space with senseless physical and psychological intimidation and bullying. Using tactics such as verbally abusing us and his children, even driving his big

RV dangerously close to us on our morning walk, ploughing its' chunky tires through our newly laid, manicured lawn seemed to be his perverted way of amusing himself. I tried my best not to become involved in their feuding, but the tediously petty bickering that developed between the two of them, the constant arguing about insignificant things, brought stress and disruption into our otherwise harmonious home, causing the two of us to argue about Ron's untenable intervention.

My every thought about him and his behaviour lit a fire in my head, ever increasing the inflammation in my mind, which eventually became a pressure cooker of mental fury. Overburdened with stress as a consequence of Ron's interference and aggression, and the sense that my loving relationship was slipping away, in this darkened state of mind, I began to imagine that people and events were conspiring to wreck my relationship and my business. My whole world felt threatened and I made some silly choices and said and did some fairly ridiculous things, things that ultimately caused me angst and cost me both friendships and money, all of which I afterwards used up much time worrying about and regretting.

Exasperated and unhappy once again, I had allowed the emotions of frustration and anger spilling from my mind to overwhelm me. My happy life had suddenly become a very dark place.

But this time, way beyond my comprehension, a far bigger picture was about to unfold, a panoramic portrait of a new way of life, one I never could have imagined, not in my wildest dreams.

Here's another question you probably didn't expect: Did you ever study Latin? You may or may not be familiar with a phrase the Romans might have used: *Felix culpa*. It translates in modern English to "fortunate error," or, if you like, a lucky mistake. Which is exactly what my unhappy experience would turn out to be because ultimately it was those out-of-control manifestations of my deepest emotions, my fears and anger, my fury that would bring me to my knees and to surrendering to change. This reoccurring, unwanted, unfortunate and unhappy event effectively forced me to undertake a comprehensive and cathartic review of the way I saw my life, a total review of my sensibilities about life, and to change my whole life paradigm.

You see, for forty-six years I'd been living in a state of *unconscious unawareness*. A state I've described as, 'living the dark'.

All this drama, this domestic upheaval, had seemingly erupted out of nowhere. Penny had seemed, to me, to be free and happy. Before I met her she and her ex had been separated for eight years. Eight years! Surely, you'd expect, they'd had time enough to put it all behind them and both be able to get on with their future lives without the need to wrangle and fight like children about such trivial matters as which of them still owned an old television set, which of them owned the family dog, whether or not their two children should be allowed to have the dog, and which of them was responsible for feeding and walking it. There were money and property issues too, things that had never been resolved, but in the main it was pretty petty stuff, all of it. Still, employing all this pettiness to great effect, they managed to perpetuate their apparent contempt for one another, and the resulting untenable misery for us all, for many months.

Understandably, their unending drama slowly but surely got under my skin. Ordinarily mundane events began to become difficult for me to manage, events such as daily business decisions and domestic issues, including those around their teenage children's attitudes towards me. Whenever I considered there was need for discipline, Penny's defence of their behaviour seemed to reflect a very biased view in favour of her children. The processes I employed to maintain peace and gain control of situations weren't working at all, and the more I tried, the worse it became. The distraction of my constantly, angrily thinking about so many tedious issues was impacting my business too. I was beginning to get a reputation for being short-tempered.

Late one evening Ron arrived abruptly and unexpectedly at our new front door, purportedly to return the old ten-inch TV that he'd "kidnapped" from Penny's workplace some weeks before. Considering my mood, he was lucky not to have it redelivered through his windscreen! The argument that ensued was the 'last straw'. After being subjected to their selfish bad behaviour and biting my tongue for nearly two years, finally, I *exploded!*

Eight hours later, Penny, her children, their personal belongings and most of the furniture were gone from the house, never to return. The end was certainly quick. But for me, emotionally, it was also very painful.

To further intensify my agonizing dilemma, my dear, elderly mother and her friend were soon due to arrive from overseas, coming to spend Christmas with us—with just me now—in what was now an almost completely empty house. Why is it that these events always occur right on Christmas? Just as the thermostat on your refrigerator fails right after you've finished loading all that festive seasonal food and wine into it. And can anyone ever find a repairman at that time of year? No, no chance!

My previous personal crisis's and unhappy relationship endings had already left their effects; emotional upset was not new to me. Despite my efforts to create a happy life, it seemed I'd chosen my life path and my partners blindly, and now this painfully intolerable and emotionally disturbing event had sent me reeling. Dumped in a serious state of shock and disbelief, I felt sickness in my stomach and utter grief for the loss of all that I thought was good, all that I'd worked so hard to achieve. Like a sudden death in the family, it seemed too quick and so wrong, and I had never felt so lonely in all my life. In this, my darkest moment, I was in dire need of a repairman, if anyone ever was.

The very next day, as if some alien force had sensed my need, a repairman, a repair*woman* in my case, miraculously appeared. I'll call her Ms M.

Ms M was Penny's older sister. I'd previously spoken with her only occasionally, so we were not all that well acquainted; however, Ms M turned out to be a woman not only of great compassion and broad life experience, but also of great spiritual depth, she seemed to project what I'd call an *inner knowing*.

Although living some distance away, she'd heard the news, and telephoned me out of concern, speaking empathetically in a calm and understanding voice. This welcome but unexpected intervention felt strangely psychic to me, for she was not expressing sympathy so much as an intuitive *knowing* about my feelings, my state of fear and grief. This was a complete surprise to me. I'd certainly never had a conversation with anyone like it before. Ms M's sudden presence in my life, right then when I needed someone to genuinely understand, was a hugely comforting relief. And, to this day, I'm so grateful that she appeared when she did, and I remain astonished at what transpired over the next hours.

You may have heard it said that there are no accidents in life, that everything has a meaning and a place. Well, it's true. I have come to know that each event and every person we encounter offers us some potential to move towards a better, deeper understanding of our life. Of course, more often than not, there's a catch. And so these opportunities will usually arrive quite unexpectedly as well as cleverly disguised. That is to say, at least until we reach a certain point in life, a point of *Self-understanding*. Only then will we see them clearly. The knack, when we do reach that point, is to acknowledge them, to be open to them, to be available for change, and to act upon them.

Unbeknownst to me, Ms M's former husband and his partner had, for twenty years, been conducting what might be called spiritual awakenings, facilitation for Self-awareness for people of all walks of life who were suffering some form of personal crisis. That crisis may have been the result of some form of psychological or personal abuse, of drug or alcohol addiction, or perhaps some financial disaster or physical illness, may have been the effects of a lifetime of *living in the dark.*

Having only met this couple socially, once or twice, I knew nothing of their work and was amazed to learn about it, to say the least. The prospect of my ever attending such an event, however, was never on my radar screen. But from my observations and the advice Ms M offered me that day, she clearly had a depth of understanding of the processes they employed. She knew my attendance was inevitable.

In her compassionately persuasive manner, she asked me to meet with her at the local surf beach. I was told to immediately drop all notions of attending business matters and forgo any reminders of what was, not so many hours ago, my happy home. To me, that part of her request sounded tempting, but emotionally I was still a train wreck and felt terribly embarrassed that others already knew of my relationship failure. The implications for my small-town business, and my life generally, were just too much to even think about. Nevertheless, as much due to Ms M's soft but persuasive insistence as to the intensity of my emotional pain, I agreed.

Flex Culpa — A fortunate Error or Happy mistake.

Exasperated and unhappy once again, I had allowed the emotions of frustration and anger spilling from my mind to overwhelm me. My life had suddenly become a very dark place.

The right people will always come into your life at the right time, for the right reason. You just have to learn to recognize those people and the reasons.

The very next day, as if some alien force had sensed my need, a repairman, a repairwoman in my case, miraculously appeared.

Chapter 2

The Happiness Secret

I found Ms M standing, waiting for me, her back turned to the powerful ocean just metres away, yet she seemed oblivious to its roar and the soft, salty sea-spray dampening her hair. As I approached, I noticed that she was holding a single long strand of grass. Greeting me with a few warm, quiet words and a brief hug, she soon handed me one end of the grass, asking me to hold onto it tightly, and then, pulling the other end back until it was taut against my grip, told me to close my eyes and to think about Penny and me back together, in our new home. She said, "Go there in your thoughts, Steve. See yourself there, and feel that feeling of love and comfort." I did.

After a minute or so, standing quietly, firmly holding the grass and thinking deeply, I began to experience a sense of relief. In fact, quite soon I felt emotionally much lighter than I had for many hours. Then, again quite unexpectedly, Ms M asked me to consciously stop those comforting thoughts and to shift my thoughts quickly and *consciously* to a completely different subject, to think about and feel now the horrible feelings I'd felt when Penny walked out, leaving me in an empty house. She said to me; "Recall as vividly as you can, those feelings you experienced when you realised you were alone and Penny wasn't coming back—ever."

With eyes still closed, I refocused my mind on the second subject. At this moment, as if to amplify my searing pain, Ms M spoke again, sincerely reminding me that my relationship was finished, lost and irretrievable.

Within seconds, my former sense of comfort in my thoughts about our happy home, was totally gone, and I was again completely overcome by strong emotions of dread and fear. That's when I broke down, shaking uncontrollably, filled again with grief and painful emotion. These felt like the worst moments in my life. Then, through my now diminished consciousness and blurred vision, I heard Ms M say; "Let go, Steve. Let go the grass. Let it go from your grip."

That day, and those few words, I will never forget. Stuck in dark emotion, it wasn't easy for me to let go. At first, I actually couldn't. It took some effort to let go, *conscious* effort. The seconds went by very slowly, ... 9, 10, 11, 12, 13, 14, 15, until eventually the grass fell from my grip.

Then, beyond any expectation, any result I could possibly have imagined, something amazing happened.

At the very same moment I let go the grass, the intensity of my emotions eased. My feelings of fear, grief, loss, and loneliness were gone, dissolved into nothing. Instantaneously. It was miraculous. What a profound experience. What a relief. What a revelation!

In my state of misery, my dark, emotional pain, I hadn't realised what a powerful force my mind was or what authority it held over me, any more than I'd realized what my holding of my end of that blade of grass had meant. You see, due to ingrained subconscious conditioning, in my mind I'd mistakenly imagined that Ms M's holding her end of the grass was her way of illustrating empathy, as if offering me her hand for comfort and support, and for a moment I was taken aback, and curious too, about why she'd so abruptly severed the connection between us.

Having unconsciously believed in and relied upon what was my subconsciously perceived sense of security, of sympathy, empathy, comfort and support created by the connection to Ms M, even via a single, fragile strand of grass, my *conscious* act of letting it go, brought about not just the jolting disconnection of that perceived security, but an instant and *conscious* recognition, the realisation that both my sense of security and my fears were not real, but perceptions of my mind.

I felt as if some huge rubber band wound up inside me had broken. Miraculously, I'd been unexpectedly and abruptly released from the strong grip of fear my mind had held over me; suddenly all the former feelings of grief and strife in me were gone, totally removed from my body and mind; and my aching heart felt light again.

Incredibly, that subconscious perception of security, of protection against my misery, my inner story of grief, had been severed in an instant. How was that possible? What was going on here, and what had happened to me?

Here's what.

Magic had happened. A profound secret of life had been revealed. And my conscious awakening was dawning.

I learned five magical truths that day, truths that relatively few people know about, and even fewer live by. Collectively these five truths reveal to us The Happiness Secret. Since having them revealed to me that day, I've always carried them with me, living by them to ensure I maintain my inner happiness. After proving their worth to me over the past twenty years, I want now to disclose them to you.

These are the truths Ms M's simple exercise had uncovered, demonstrating concisely and overpoweringly these little-known but universally applied realities:

- That we create in our subconscious minds, a *perception* of all our life events from which we derive our many states of being, states such as terror or joy, freedom or failure, and
- That we most often, unconsciously, allow ourselves to become totally persuaded by and reliant upon, our minds *perception*, and
- That bringing to mind and intensely focusing our thoughts, on any of those perceptions that cause us emotional anguish, then quickly and *consciously*

shifting our thoughts to another, non-anguishing, subject, reveals to us a clear and concise illustration of one of life's greatest secrets, which is

- That our emotional state at any time is entirely the product of and directly connected to our thoughts in the same moment.

If this mere shard of advice sounds too simple or insignificant to be of any great value to you, then take a moment to consider the predictable conclusion; the fifth and most definitive truth uncovered.

- That if we can learn to understand and control our subconscious mind, we can, consequently, control and ultimately erase our emotional pain. Our unhappiness.

Read and understand this advice as meaning *your* subconscious mind's perceptions, your conscious thoughts and your emotional pain. Of course as a consequence of this understanding, you will also have learned how to control your actions and behaviour.

Now you can make this knowledge your own Happiness Secret, to have and to hold forever, to fully understand its power, and to use to maintain control in your head and create enduring happiness in your life.

In the upcoming chapters you will learn how to apply the Happiness Secret to everyday issues and towards achieving enduring happiness in your life.

I urge you to not take this profound and precious information lightly.

"So," I hear you say, "okay. I get it, but exactly how will this help me to achieve my inner happiness? And will it in fact work for me?" To which I can only reply, yes it will, given your own *conscious* commitment and your performance of a simple exercise. But for now, I ask that you reserve your judgement until you've read this book right through to the end, by which time you'll not want to make any judgements about anything at all.

Here's this amazing secret revealed to you again:

Consciously changing your thoughts causes your emotions to change instantly, simultaneously.

You may consider this not such a big deal. You'll consider that we already change our minds and review our thoughts thousands of times every day. We do. The difference is that we're not usually aware of any effect it might have on us, because;

1. We are not generally dealing with what might be deemed emotionally disturbing events,

and

2. Such thoughts and mind changes are made unconsciously, automatically. They are seldom conscious.

Accordingly, in our day-to-day thinking, depending upon the subject, the intensity of our thoughts and emotions will range widely.

Let's say if we mark these most common, normal, and varying emotions on a graph showing their effects in emotional degrees, they'd be mid- range. i.e. from high low degrees to low high degrees, because these everyday emotions don't generally trouble us much at all, whereas extreme or intense emotions do.

We'd accordingly mark more extreme emotions on the graph as being either very low degree—where we might become depressed—or very high degree, where we might scream or lose our temper —we might explode!

Consequently, we accept without questioning the results of our everyday, automatic, mid-range or 'middle-of-the-road' mind changes and the automatic, 'middle-of-the-road' results that occur. And we similarly accept that when we're depressed or angered that those conditions too are emotions that are the result of life's effects on us. We accept that that's how life is.

I'm sure you'll relate to this and to another common human trait, one whereupon living in a relatively safe world with every modern convenience at our disposal, we can be terrible procrastinators, deferring our need to *consciously* enquire about knowledge for many aspects of life until we desperately *have to know* ... or until we're embedded in some crisis. And when that crisis arrives, of course we are just far too unprepared. We find ourselves at a loss to cope or to manage.

It's in the midst of such a crisis that we most often react inappropriately, even explode emotionally and *unconsciously*. When our emotions change dramatically, causing unexpected behaviour, resulting in equally dramatically changed interaction with others, we quickly find ourselves in a state of fearfulness, of self-doubt. Even deep misery can arise and overwhelm us, sometimes staying long enough for us to experience deep sorrow and regret and, with that, an acute state of unhappiness.

So let's be quite clear about this. In times of crisis, allowing our usually unconsidered or unconscious choices to lead us is *not* the way to happiness. On the contrary, this action is best described as living by chance or by the seat of your pants. Not only is it not a plan for happiness, it's not how your life should ever be.

Ironically, though, it's these very same catastrophes, arisen from unconsciously derived "wrong choices" that can present us with our greatest opportunities to make profound changes in our lives. That's right, it's actually those *Felix culpa* events that can move us from our misery to happiness, and move us in an instant. Had I had this knowledge prior to the time of my life crisis, I'd have called up Ron and said, "Bring on the drama, bring it on, please!" Of course I didn't, but how very fortunate that he brought it to me anyway. I explain how he did, in a later chapter.

Experience has shown me that we should always expect the unexpected, such miraculous events as the right people always coming into your life at the right time, for the right reason. We just have to learn to recognise the people, and the reasons, at the time. When next there's an unhappy crisis in your life—perhaps you're experiencing one right now—you too should say, "Bring it on." As was the case for me, your own greatest life crisis could quite unexpectedly become your portal into a whole new world, a portal into a world of enduring happiness.

In the chapters ahead we'll uncover the truth about perceived *unhappiness*, learn how misery can be the best means to happiness, and discover more about what enduring happiness really is and how to achieve it.

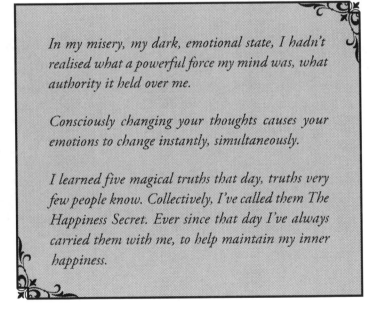

In my misery, my dark, emotional state, I hadn't realised what a powerful force my mind was, what authority it held over me.

Consciously changing your thoughts causes your emotions to change instantly, simultaneously.

I learned five magical truths that day, truths very few people know. Collectively, I've called them The Happiness Secret. Ever since that day I've always carried them with me, to help maintain my inner happiness.

CHAPTER 3

Our Unhappy World

Likely you have acquired this book because either you or someone you love is experiencing some form of unhappiness. Please don't feel that you, or they, are alone. Hardly a living person does not suffer from emotional turmoil, from fear or angst. Why else would we say, "Rest in peace" when a person dies? Clearly, we're acknowledging that their life on earth was hindered by unhappy events and not free from sorrow or pain. What we're really saying is "Finally you're now free from emotional pain!" But is it not too late to say this after they've died? Should we not all have had happiness throughout life and not have to wait for death to be at peace? Of course we should. But, due to our modern lifestyles, our in-built beliefs and subsequent "thinking," like influenza, this twenty-first-century human condition we call unhappiness is a common and debilitating condition, and it's universal. It is, in fact, considering all its forms, the most prevalent emotional disorder within the human race. And its negative impact on people's lives should not be underestimated.

Unhappiness is the illness or disorder we know least about, speak least about, and do the least to resolve and to reverse. Yet it's surely the one disorder we should know most about and do most about, since its worldwide prevalence is eroding the foundations of the lives of hundreds of millions of people, all of us citizens of this all-too-often unhappy world, we of all walks of life, all nationalities, all socioeconomic status and religious persuasions, who have never stopped to consider *why* we're unhappy, and why unhappiness is so prevalent. Yet we must. And we must *understand* why it is, so we can conquer it, before it manifests as something much worse.

Surely, you must be thinking, *there must be some common denominator at work here, some human gene, perhaps. How else could one human condition become so widespread?* Well, yes, there is. The common denominator, which is just as subtly and ingeniously hidden as your DNA code, is in your brain. It is your subconscious mind, unconsciously thinking and continuously influencing your emotions and behaviour.

You see, what is least understood about our unhappiness—due entirely to the fact that this knowledge is not commonly taught—is that our unhappiness is the product of our subconscious preconditioning. That is to say, our subconscious minds archived thoughts in relation to our life experiences. Even more succinctly, it's our inability to stop our subconscious thoughts in their tracks, whenever they begin to direct our behaviour, and our life choices. Without acquiring knowledge about our subconscious thoughts, we're unable to control them through fully understanding what they really are and where they come from.

In the main, throughout our lives, we have never given much consideration to what our any of thoughts are or to from where they arise nor to what it is that ignites them. We have neither considered which of our thoughts most detrimentally affect our lives by negatively stimulating our emotions nor why they do. And we haven't been effective in addressing or understanding this matter because, frankly, we're constantly *thinking*. Yes, thinking, which some might consider a harmless activity, but we're usually thinking about the world outside of our mind, seldom, if ever, about the world within it. And we are irrepressible thinkers; like an engine that never runs out of fuel, we never ever stop thinking. Even as you read this, try not to be thinking about anything, even for a second!

The fact is that we have layer upon layer of thoughts streaming continuously, ever revolving in our heads, 24/7. Our brain activity is, of course, vital, so it's obviously been going on for a very long time, since the beginnings of humankind. And through all that time, humankind has been prone to suffering. Why? Because the most critical aspect of ourselves, our *conscious awakening*, is missing. So it is our conscious awakening that we must develop if we're to gain control of suffering and replace it with enduring happiness.

You see, whilst our constant thinking may keep us awake at night, it keeps our awakening asleep!

We should ask ourselves, "How can this circumstance still be, in this, the twenty-first century?" We should also ask ourselves, if our uncontrolled thinking can have such a negative impact on our happiness in life, then why have we never learned effective ways to manage it, to manage our thoughts and emotions in order to avoid unwanted issues such as debilitating suffering? Surely this subject should have been an integral part of our early education. Why today are we *still* not taught these fundamental life skills in schools or in churches? And why not even in our homes?

You know, if we're honest about it, most of us haven't been taught how to manage our diets or our money either! We should instantly recognise these two very common thought subjects as prime causes for many people's unhappiness. And they're just two of the thousands of challenging subjects that occupy our minds. Let's take the time to reflect in this chapter on our unhappy world, uncovering some reasons, *cleverly hidden in your subconscious,* that you might identify as the causes of your own unhappiness or that of your loved ones. After all, there are so many possibilities, and if you are to win your battle in this war with unhappiness you'd better get to know and understand your enemy.

You'll agree that, all things considered, despite our early years having been our most formative, when our young minds were evolving, were like sponges for knowledge, we were actually taught almost nothing in the way of life skills at our schools, universities, and churches. But have you ever wondered why? The simple answer is; it doesn't behove or benefit those institutions to teach such skills. Believe it or not, it's not even core to their teachings, the methodologies of which are primarily based in students having to *engage* their minds, to memorize and to think. But, at this early age and having little life experience upon which to draw and reflect, most young students are blindly engaged in the schools' or churches' specific curricula, which themselves demand compliance, effort, and mindfulness.

Modern education is all about excelling academically. It's where scholastic achievement is offered the promise of reward of a higher status within life and one's community. And not just for students, but more and more for the school itself, for its rank in the government education system's and society's 'pecking order', where schools are compared one with another within the community as to which is the best for parents to place their children, to ensure they succeed in life. This clearly is the case when parents will give preference to a school as much as for its social standing as for its capacity to provide their children with a rounded education. However, instead of ever-higher achievement, the outcomes of many educational systems too often reflect falling levels of student competency but rising levels of anxiety. This anxiety is not restricted to school-leaving age, but continues on, right through the lives of many young men and women, because the events of the stressful formative years are locked into their subconscious minds.

In the meantime, operating like so many growing businesses chasing market share, many universities, schools and churches have become monumental business enterprises, accumulating valuable real estate holdings and serious wealth. Materially and financially, they're loaded, and schoolrooms are loaded too, with equipment and technology, which one would hope would lead to higher levels of academic attainment. But despite all this technological collateral, or perhaps because of it, today's students are subjected to more and more pressure. Firstly, there's peer pressure - to have the latest electronic devices that others have – in addition to those provided by schools. Next is community pressure, societies expectation of their *need to succeed* academically in order to achieve a high social and employment status. The school too might bring pressure upon students to maintain and enhance its own social and economic status.

But all this modern technology hasn't compensated for the lack of a fundamental understanding within our learning institutions, that all students of all academic capabilities, first and foremost, need happiness in their lives, to be happy within themselves. After all, won't a happy student, a happy person, always do well? Because, the effects of happiness radiating outwards, to others and the to world in general, reflect back most beneficially to those who exude them.

Our modern educational institutes' almost total disregard for a students' spiritual development (not to be confused with any religious teaching), that is to say, their disregard for any notion of the Self or attainment of Self-knowledge (not to be confused with human psychology), is a serious omission in all western world educational institutions' curricula.

While churches have always promoted their particular beliefs or ideologies, and schools their own curricula and teaching methodologies, what has historically been so detrimental about the methods used by these institutions, supposedly for the attainment of academic accomplishment and social acceptance of their students, is that they have all subtly but skilfully employed *fear* as a whip.

For example, to achieve their own ends, churches the world- over have for six hundred-odd years, deliberately and unashamedly employed fear of retribution, annihilation in some invented hell, an afterlife reprimand for failure or conversely, the promise of reward for compliance, by their invented deity, their particular interpretation of 'God'. It's extraordinary that this manipulation of minds remains morally acceptable and legal in the twenty-first century, yet it survives and is seemingly just as effective as it was 600 years ago. Schools, too, under the guidance of governments keen to apply uniformity, perhaps for the purpose of maintaining economic control as much as to ensure wide community education, have just as skilfully used fear to persuade. Fear of academic failure is a powerful means to achieve results, constantly comparing ones' self against the achievements of others can be an unnerving process. These unjust, draconian methods embed indelible notions of life's expectations of a persons levels of ability leading to doubt, suspicion, dread, and anxiety in young subconscious minds, quite possibly restricting, even suffocating, the potential of a full and happy life for hundreds of millions of young people.

The implementation of such onerous, even exploitive, teaching methodologies combined with inflexible end-of-term exam' design requiring strict student compliance, and the subsequent convoluted marking methodologies, are measures that may work favourably for the school and perhaps for some students, but not necessarily for all.

It's a fact that exam results are not a true measure of a student's worth, yet many students, intimidated by these daunting and inflexible examination and scoring systems, consequently don't perform as well as they might otherwise. In this highly competitive and socially sophisticated world, such "failure" might easily result in a student's perception of social disgrace and collapsed career prospects. Particularly in todays social-media influenced world, a young persons' not meeting subconsciously imposed self-expectation may have dire results. Notwithstanding that corporal punishment was banished many years ago, these psychologically effected fear tactics remain a crushingly powerful means of influencing and controlling very young minds. As a set of guidelines for living they are clearly inappropriate, restricting an individuals' freedom to develop, and are a very poor foundation upon which any person could expect to build a life paradigm comprising truth, trust and happiness.

Conversely, education programs emphasising *Self*-awareness and *Self*-understanding as underlying fundamentals to a successful, happy life, would give reason, understanding and balance to a young person's life expectations. Then universally, education outcomes would much better reflect a students abilities, strengths, and accomplishment propensities. These kinds of programs would provide far more reliable guidance, enhancing the chances for a happy future as well as an appropriate career.

Sadly today, in far too many homes, traditional parental guidance is diminished or has completely failed as the many differing and ever-compounding aspects of modern-day social and domestic life take precedence over teaching children life skills and self-knowledge. What was once the dining table discussion where family storytelling, the interchange of moral and cultural ideas, took place between generations, has dissolved into family silence in front of a television set, or separated family members staring at separate screens, in separate rooms. Meals are no longer eaten at the dining table, but on the coffee table, desk, bed, or floor.

Headphones are worn to block out each other, and the real world.

These seemingly harmless but divisive trends have crept into our homes and communities almost without our noticing. Society has opted now to simply label people by age group, differentiating recent past generations for having distinctly different values, personal idiosyncrasies, different sensibilities and aspirations from one another – Gen X (those born 1963 to 1980) Gen Y, (1981 to 1994) Gen Z (1995 to 2009) and now it's Generation Alpha (post 2010). No longer a cohesive people, we're now pigeon holed like spare parts in a factory storeroom.

It's clear that an ever-widening gap has opened between generations, but also between siblings of differing ages, and between parents and children, diminishing personal contact. When family members don't speak to one another, how can a child feel able to openly discuss a troublesome issue? Parents encouragement and application to teaching children to apply quiet *Self*-reflection to resolving the sort of troubling event that might arise in the mind of a younger child or teenager, no longer gets the consideration it deserves. And many serious issues do arise in the home, quite possibly *due* to children having become more isolated than ever. In summary, you might say that people have lost their power for self-vigilance, for monitoring the quality of their lives. As wonderfully interactively entertaining as they may be, electronic communications devices can never replace or supersede conscious, personal human interaction.

In our so called, developed and wealthy western world, millions of children come home from school to an empty house while both parents work to meet the mortgage payments on the residential monument they call home, a dwelling they're seldom *at home* in, and that some may never actually own, ever. You may say; "But they're aspiring to, they're working to, own it." In response, I ask, "But at what cost?"

When reflecting on this issue, we should ask ourselves:

- What measuring stick did they use when they decided to undertake two full-time careers to meet payments on the mortgage required to purchase it?
- What were *their* life-management skills?
- What were their priorities?
- What value did they put upon a happy family life?

These questions are especially relevant at this time, in our twenty-first century, when the biggest global credit bubble in history brought about a situation whereby people quite falsely believed that they're wealthy, that they could afford anything they wanted. While there may be nothing wrong with people aspiring, they should, nevertheless, have applied more meaningful consideration to the potential consequences of overextending their capabilities to reach what material things they came to believe they should possess if they were to live happier lives.

In no short measure, it's because of this great twenty-first-century folly that we witnessed the most elaborate and disastrous worldwide financial crisis in history, the so-called GFC, (global financial crisis) the *bursting* of that credit bubble that we all were reliant upon. So disastrous a crisis was it, that some of world's biggest national economies are left in dire straits, their booming economies smouldering as the highly unethical, arguably illegal, but certainly technically and structurally sophisticated, financial lending and investment structures collapsed. These were structures devised by greedy financial lending institutions, corporations determined to harness and entrap the uninitiated, the most vulnerable, those millions of unconscious people whose expectations of a life of material wealth had been embedded in them by other, equally greedy corporations, those promoting the sale of material goods and the convoluted methods for acquiring them. Binding contracts for providing credit or finance to millions who could never afford to repay the debt they incurred, were issued recklessly by banks and lending institutions the world over. That debt then sold in turn to other corporations at discounted values to alleviate the risk of the initial lenders. The trail of contracts, corporations and responsibilities became so complex and elaborate that even the worlds' most powerful governments could not unravel them. Some of the biggest and most unethical corporations, having been determined by non-vigilant governments to be 'too big to allow them to fall', have been propped up by the very tax-payers who were fleeced of their savings and after tax income, further burdening those already financially overwhelmed by the wrong doing. Today, new and much tougher measures on lending, much stricter loan qualification criteria, introduced to prevent further high-risk lending, means most borrowers cannot afford to buy back their homes, or a new home to replace the one they've lost.

As a consequence, millions have been left homeless, destitute, unemployed and without hope of ever regaining the lifestyle they were tricked into believing was possible, perhaps ever.

In the aftermath of this corporate and government money making recklessness, many countries' economies remain in serious jeopardy of fiscal ruin; Britain, Ireland, Spain, Greece and Portugal to name just some of those most affected. The USA's national debt level also completely out of control, many trillions of dollars of debt, ever rising, at the rate of tens of thousands of dollars per second! This may sound unbelievable, incomprehensible, but it's true. Big, formerly socially and financially healthy cities in the United States have filed for bankruptcy. And all this monetary mayhem is due entirely to a world culture of material greed and to blind, corrupt, and self-serving businessmen and their corporations, allowed to run riot by apathetic national governance. As is much unhappiness, too.

In our own apathy, our state of unconsciousness, nonchalantly naming the event, the GFC. we're all left financially and socially, reeling, wondering; *What the heck happened! Why are tens of millions suddenly out of work, and millions more homeless? How, and to where, did all the apparent wealth disappear? Why did we not see such a crisis coming?*

The truth is, you would have to admit, that we didn't *want* to see it coming; the whole greedy western world didn't *want* to know. It wasn't what we *believed* the world owed us or would deliver to us. We all *believed* we were *entitled* to wealth. Well then, wouldn't you recommend that we should all stop *believing and wanting*, and develop a sense of *knowing*, and make more *conscious*, more intelligent choices about our personal, social and business morals and values from there? Should we not develop true happiness in our lives through applying more *conscious awareness in our lives, and not through blindly pursuing the acquisition of material things?* We'd know better then what future circumstances we could expect. We'd *know,* not to have *any* expectations.

In a later chapter, you'll learn how you can leave old wanting and believing behind you, and come to knowing, through conscious awareness.

It's so important to our building a life of happiness and contentment that we 'get' this; that we develop our understanding of our world from truthful, conscious stance. After all, it's a world we've grown up in and have hope to rely upon for our lives' successful, safe, and happy unfolding. Growing up and happiness do and must go hand in hand. But these two are not states of being that every one of us achieves. The influences within our modern materialistic culture, blindly marching forward, are making such achievement more and more difficult for many. If we're to lead truly happier lives, we need to learn how to manage modern life and the pressures and demands it bestows upon us, to understand that the best, most enduring and all-encompassing way to achieve that, is to learn about and to understand the nature of our preconditioned subconscious minds. Only then will we have the chance to develop the new habit of making intellectually *conscious* decisions about all life matters, and not allow our lives to be influenced by subconscious conditioning, or the trickery of greedy corporations!

That we've missed out on important lessons in life management doesn't usually dawn upon us until long after we've left college and university, but it can land hard when we're married with children and have a mortgage or are out of work, those times when our personal relationships and financial and emotional security are at risk. Only then we may or may not realise that we'd better learn and quickly, lest the very fabric of our lives and that of our families become undone.

Throughout the western world recent studies of modern lifestyles show high levels of financial over-commitment; and of ill health due to poor diet, and to tobacco, illicit drug and alcohol addiction; of increasing rates of obesity, depression and suicide in both younger and older generations, most often brought about by stress. So much of this stress arising from everyday events such as bullying at school and in the workplace, by unemployment and financial overburden, homes and family farms being repossessed by banks, and by the ever-increasing neglect and dysfunction within family structure.

Reports of the effects of child abuse, alarmingly and notoriously too often committed within the protection of a government, religious, or educational institution, are common bad news. The only good news being that around the world, victims' cries for acknowledgement and genuine help have finally brought appropriate action. Under a tidal wave of public outrage, governments have been forced to intervene. Over-riding church and institutional self-regulation, enlightened governments are at last properly investigating the thousands of cases of child abuse swept under the carpet by various church and other educational institutional leaders, whose primary objective reverted to protecting not the abused children in their care, but protecting their institutions' undeserving reputations. That such wealthy organisations when found guilty, would argue vigorously about the cost of compensation for the victims of their crimes, is even more violation, further diminishing their social standing.

Consider for a moment the emotional misery suffered by thousands of families subjected to the loss of children through suicide due to abuse. Consider the unhappiness, distress and suffering of the thousands victims themselves in their shocking realisation that the institution or church they so deeply believed in and depended upon was so recklessly managed, and abhorrently infiltrated by paedophiles. It's understandable that both the parents involved and the victims themselves were all certain they would be afforded the best chance of developing a happy and successful life under the guidance of those institutions and the supposedly honourable people who ran them. Yet clearly, they could not have been further misled.

Such a breakdown in morality in that part of society held highest would have seemed to them incomprehensible. Likewise those millions of folks whose overpriced homes were repossessed when they failed to meet their unaffordable mortgage payments. So many of who found themselves out in the street, or worse.

On reflection, you would have to agree that they all would wish to have had the means within themselves to decide their own fates. But without that means, without *Self*-knowledge, the means to make *conscious* decisions, they could only instead rely upon directions given by others which were horribly flawed and guided them not into the safe harbour of knowledge, love, harmony and a home, but directly onto the rocks of abuse and certain emotional and financial demise. Only in time and with the achievement, universally, of humankinds inherent ability to apply *conscious awareness,* which *is* vested in *all* of us, will we ever reach the point where self-determination, self-actualization, will be every person's choice.

Seemingly beyond us in our times of unhappiness, that achievement, like mans' first walk on the moon, is nonetheless coming 'one small step at a time'. And your own opportunity to play your part, by developing and embracing your own conscious awareness, is directly ahead of you. So perhaps you should read on.

It's undeniable that the abhorrent abuse issues just described are difficult for many church followers to come to terms with. Such justifiably strong doubts about their teachings by churches, of their long held beliefs, must be unsettling. Many must be plagued by thoughts of just to whom and to where they should turn for spiritual and emotional support. Those unconscionable acts of crime, committed against innocents, are undeniable, indefensible and were far too commonplace. Worse, that this knowledge, as well as that of so many, thought trustworthy, lending institutions unethical misconduct, seemed only to become public knowledge and all too apparent to our government authorities after the fact, after the damage was done, begs the question: just how on earth has our society and our culture brought us to this sad situation? Why did we not see these worldwide social and financial catastrophes coming? Are we so blind?

In a word, yes. As a people, due to our widely spread cultures of blind beliefs, of desire for material wealth, power, and money, and for striving, we have become internally blind. And we defer responsibility for happiness in our lives much too often, to others. Worse still, we are in the main, intellectually, *totally unaware* of this endemic twenty-first-century cultural curse. Taught to expect, and to achieve more and more, we are conversely too egocentric, too externally driven, by material wanting and consumption, to give matters other than our own egotistical self-importance the slightest consideration. And so we suffer. Unhappiness abounds.

Despite our "education," we have never properly been taught what's right and what's wrong within our lifestyles. Today, 'anything goes'. We are more fiercely intent on measuring our happiness in terms of our material and personal wealth, and by what we deem our successful, interpersonal connectivity with others - now too often conducted only by texting or tweeting – in the hope of developing a "following" of "friends," as if, for example, having hundreds or even thousands of Facebook friends is supposed to be important and meaningful. Whatever happened to speaking to one another, person-to-person and getting together with family members and genuine friends?

Addiction to and reliance upon these technological means of communication has us leaning more and more towards living in a virtual world and in social solitude, becoming less compassionate, less connected and more psychologically alone because we're more physically detached from one another. We're effectively relating to, and relying upon machines, more so than people for our social interaction, making it difficult to measure or ascertain the real value in, and meaning of, personal relationships. Is it an inner emptiness, a lack of self esteem and psychological security or simply a need for attention, for validation of their existence, that millions of people post their personal details on social media sites for all the whole world to view? Clicking "Like" or inviting strangers to become "friends" - to 'follow' you by joining your page on social media vehicles like Facebook, for example - clearly risks a degree of personal security. The obvious fragility of such "friendships" demonstrates that they're hardly sincere, yet many people apparently associate themselves more closely with the so-called social media celebrities or television and film characters they 'meet' by these means, than with their own family members, their neighbours, or the people within their community, where sincere friends, and a truer sense of self-worth would be found.

Miraculous as it is, the Internet or world-wide-web, seems a cold and inhumane, even a dangerous means for communicating one's personal feelings, perhaps particularly if posting personal details and photographic images of oneself in the hope of attracting the attention of some stranger, a practice proven to have been socially disastrous when merciless 'revenge attacks' by heartless individuals have punished such acts of naivety with psychological cruelty. When your written communications are conducted via texting, and the use of the English language, its alphabet, letters and punctuation is purely arbitrary, it's likely that your message might be misinterpreted, hijacked, or abused.

Of course you may consider that this social media stuff is all purely in fun, for a laugh. Yet every year, tens of thousands of innocent Internet users are left emotionally and financially robbed or deprived by callous "cyber-thieves' who've tricked them into parting with their love and their money. Some people have been physically harmed, some murdered, by the demented respondents they've attracted. You'd surely have to ask yourself; *What value have I put on my life's savings, my personal dignity, my safety and relationships, that I would offer myself via the internet to complete strangers?*

The reason there is greater disillusionment, misunderstanding and unhappiness in the world is obvious. It's because there's less conscious awareness in the world.

Too many people today are deluded, and much less consciously connected to others or to reality, including the reality of meaningful personal relationships through eye-to-eye contact, personal touch, and the spoken word. Posting a smiley face does not equal a physical hug. Nor does unconsciously clicking "Like" equal reassuringly softly spoken words of understanding and advice. Cases of psychological and financial damage resulting from social media participation are mostly due to people having made reckless and regrettable, *unconscious* choices. Only the marketing companies mining the information unconsciously posted on social media sites benefit from the exercise, while the unconscious contributors' delusion of momentary 'fame' is unpaid, and can surely only be short-lived.

Compounding our unhappiness over recent years, the commodification of our needs has converted them into desires (meaning there's been a metamorphic transformation of commodities, such as housing, fashion, home products, vehicles, goods and communications devices and services, into desirable pleasures or fantasies).

To acquire these pleasures, we've embarked upon mass indulgence in purchasing using 'plastic' credit - money we don't yet have. We humorously call this foolishness, retail therapy. But it's really uncontrolled reaction in response to ever more sophisticated advertising; contrived and often false messages telling us how happy we'll be if only we would acquire certain material things. It is however, therapy that too often results in personal financial over-commitment.

Our chronic addiction to consumerism has become an integral part of our unhappy lives. In short, our moral and material values have become over-influenced and undermined by twenty-first-century corporate greed. Given our supposed intelligence, this seems inexcusable madness, yet it's endemic.

In this paradoxical twist of fate, our pursuit of happiness has brought about our unhappiness!

This use of shallow material values as a measuring stick for a happy and balanced life has brought to us an endless assortment of opportunities to feel bad about ourselves. To feel neglected or that we have less or are in some way inferior, that we've been short-changed and are generally less fortunate than we, in our deluded unconscious state, expected to be. When people's expectations are so high, and their sense of entitlement so real, they are susceptible to becoming sad and disillusioned. In the future, from that sadness and disillusionment will arise their negative *subconscious*, which recreates past negative events that can only reaffirm a persons' already ingrained perception of what failure is. Consequently, an even greater depth of unhappiness manifests. But, given their lack of *conscious awareness*, whatever else could they have expected?

If they only they had learned in their formative years to engage conscious awareness, they would as adults, not been influenced by corporate adverting fantasy. Realising the likely repercussions of financial over-indulgence, they could instead have evaded those desires and expectations, that sense of entitlement, and would never have become so disappointed, so unhappy. It's clearly an unwinnable case; amassing material wealth, on its' own won't ever equal emotional stability or enduring happiness.

All this unfortunate cultural conditioning could so easily be reversed if only we were to implement less social and material values, and, in addition to literal mathematical, mechanical and scientific academia, included more *Self-understanding*-oriented learning to early education, thereby addressing this universal *unconsciousness syndrome* at its embryonic stage. An early education curriculum might teach *Self-enlightenment and Self-knowledge*, beginning in the first year of school. In future, parents could apply curriculum at home perhaps by reading children books about *Self* and truth, instead of, at one end of the spectrum, fairy tales, or at the other end, material gain and aggression. Children today are too often subjected to entertainment much less about witches and fire breathing dragons or boys-own adventure, as about realistic computer games steeped in violence, killing and dishonesty. These are not harmless fairy tales but potentially negatively influential blueprints for a life of unhappiness.

It seems today, that there is little if any *Self*-understanding taught at all in our teaching institutions, too few fundamental life skills.

Making further and significant contribution to unhappiness in the world, our media simply saturate us with misery and negativity. The daily 'world news' has little impartial informative content but plenty of speculative comment, with a strong emphasis on the suffering in the world. It seems it's all bad news. The media go to great lengths to find that story of misery and the more personal the misery, the more commercial they consider it to be. Private family disputes, for example, are now considered newsworthy. They're made into T.V. 'reality' shows that normalize shocking, senseless behaviour and broadcast to an ever-hungry, *unconsciously unaware*, television audience to watch in the comfort of their own—unhappy—homes!

Popular television productions depict road rage, physical violence, filthy homes, and dysfunctional families, including those of so-called celebrities, and wretched children whose parents ought never have been allowed to foster them. Too many programs depict serious obesity, crime, mayhem, and murder as exciting entertainment. Such disturbing productions are standards and broadcast in the same mix as cooking contest and home-renovation shows, preceded only by, too often unheeded, parental guidance warnings. Filming criminals in action - uncouth morons behaving badly - in real-life Cop shows, is our television media's way of attracting ever-higher advertising revenues, there being no other reason to broadcast it. Sadly, this mind-numbing trash, swamping our TV screens every day and every night is nonchalantly accepted, soaked up by an audience of hundreds of millions of *unconscious* home – viewers.

What utter garbage it all is, and what deplorable role models the players in these shows make for young viewers, for us all. Yet it is well within the power of the media, desperate for revenue as they may be, to choose to start afresh, or perhaps they should be required to as a condition of their holding a broadcasting license.

With stricter, more appropriate entertainment standards, and by adopting far more appropriate measures for what they deem 'celebrity' status, before bestowing this privilege upon the frequently immoral and outrageously behaved 'stars' of the entertainment industry, those who are sought after by the media specifically for their 'shock and awe' value, they could instead, celebrate and broadcast material from the far greater volume of successful achievement, the wonderful, the good and the right that occurs every day, somewhere in our world. This course might well revitalize their viewers sense of being entertained, leading the media toward meeting the goals their industry values most, their much acclaimed 'viewer ratings' positions, may even arrest the decline in television viewer numbers and assist T.V. broadcasters in succeeding financially. With many broadcasters often struggling to survive, it's clear that their current programing formula isn't working well. Some Good News channels may well succeed where those broadcasting bad news, murder and mayhem, cannot.

Of course, the natural world provides the media with its own comprehensive daily dose of depression, desolation, gloom, wretchedness, despair, sorrow, grief, misfortune, sadness, and personal distress. Some of it is born of nature's cruelty, including droughts and famine, earthquakes and tsunamis, but thanks to weak and corrupt international leaders, there's also worldwide mayhem, terrorism bringing misery to millions, arrogant despots perpetuating crude, medieval-type civil crisis in modern cities. These numerous, unending, expensive and senseless wars are almost gleefully reported on by the media, including graphic vision of horrific deaths and maiming, in particular stories of thousands of innocent civilian lives lost. And of course there's plenty of misery and corruption found in sports and business circles, and in politics. The media never have to look far for grist for their mill.

Our politicians too, serve up an endless litany of melancholy, most often softened by promises they never mean to keep, followed by hollow apologies for why it's all gone wrong. Considering the state of our world, it's clear that the people we vest so much power and authority in, are not serving us well. We nevertheless blindly vote again at the next election. You may well ask if they wanted our support, why they would serve up this river of gloom and negativity. Why so many of them are found to be corrupt. They show no evidence of changing their personal habits, policies, campaign themes or political strategies.

So why do we put up with it, why watch and listen to it? What on earth are we thinking? (And, you might enquire, what are our government censors looking for when they rate some television productions as suitable or not, for an audience of any age?) The answer is; although we ourselves don't always understand, politicians and the media certainly do understand the complexities within our psyches. The composition, or fabrication, of their visual and verbal offerings is cleverly designed to fully harvest our fears. That is to say, it all projects toward us what they know we fear most, what we've been taught to fear from childhood and throughout our lives. They know how to push our buttons. Unwittingly, we've actually paid them to analyse us, by which means they've discovered our weaknesses. Consequently, by this means they've become totally authoritarian and unaccountable whilst impervious to our real needs. And they effectively use this knowledge to manipulate us.

But how on earth, as a world community, have we become so easily manipulated?

In our *unconscious* state, what *compels* us to follow, to read newspapers, to listen and to watch our television screens *is our great subconscious fears* nagging at us, telling us that all that badness and misery could actually so easily manifest in our own lives, in our own communities.

Because according to our nagging subconscious, our mind full of fears, it's not only all too possible, it's probable.

We fear and believe that taxes and housing costs could rise! We fear losing our jobs, and we believe that there may be a terrorist, a paedophile, or a murderer living in our street. We have been swayed by a hugely popular movie to believe that if we dared to go swimming we may be attacked and eaten by a 40 foot Great White shark! And that our kids might miss out on a good education if we don't buy a home in *that* suburb, that they might be abducted in the street if we don't drive them to school in an outsized R.V. The banks could foreclose on our mortgages! And, of course, we could be losing money if we don't grab that advertised bargain, today! Because they know our health is of particular concern to us we're targeted for fitness and renewed youth solutions, badgered to buy 'health insurance', whatever that is. It's an industry that thrives on peoples' fear of illness that pays for the advertisements!

But of course every solution offered has its price tag, and every special offer is for a *limited* period only, every product *new* and improved. It's as if what was just fine last month is now junk, out-dated and in need of replacement. Our Telco services, our appliances, cars, furniture, homes and even our mortgages must surely be out-dated! All the while, the developed world has become one huge factory churning out disposable junk with a use-by date stamped on the bottom. Just count how many household appliances, mobile or cell phones, tablets, and laptop computers you have bought and disposed of in the past ten years. You'll find your "old" ones in a cupboard somewhere, most likely in perfect working condition. And how many vehicles?

Millions of garages have no room for the vehicles intended to be parked in them since they are crammed in to their ceilings with 'stuff' bought on credit and quite possibly never unpacked. Sports equipment, bikes, scooters, clothing, shoes, electronics, tools and other never going to be used equipment, all costing money that wasn't yet earned. It's a crystal-clear demonstration of internal blindness, and a sad reflection on the value people place on their hard earned salaries. We have to ask ourselves; do we really need all this stuff in our lives, or are we simply stroking our egos, surrounding ourselves with material goods to make us appear and feel happy, and 'comfortably off'? Because, when our credit card maxes out, when some particular but temporary desire we held is satiated, unhappiness descends! When storage space runs out we rush to sell off our unwanted belongings at yard sales or offer our junk on E Bay - for a quarter of the price we paid! We're all guilty to some degree! It would be funny if it weren't so tragic.

The young and single, most often still in their teens, are targeted with tempting offers of delicious fast-food, super-thin, super-fast, multifunctional notebooks, tablets, and mobile cell phones, all of which are totally reliant upon us *consumers*, as we have come be known, signing up to convoluted agreements to purchase or lease the goods and services, such as those offered by Telco providers - called bundles or deals—but which are actually legally binding contracts contrived by corporate lawyers. We've come to learn to our detriment that these companies are far more focused on profits and shareholder dividends than on the provision or quality of the goods and services their marketing activities have misled us into believing we would receive. Government authorities, meantime, receive millions of consumer complaints daily about misleading advertising, unethical, unprofessional and illegal business practices. Yet, unconsciously, we consumers continue to consume. Like so many other modern day activities, and despite some knowledge of the pitfalls further down the road, for many people shopping and spending is simply habitual.

Let's not leave off our list for inviting misery, the hard-to-pass-up dating-site memberships offered to all ages and genders, where lonely or unhappy people are assured they'll find those ever-elusive commodities: true love, soul mates, and happiness! They make it all seem so plausible, so believable. Even those of us who don't participate are likely to think we've been short changed, that a better relationship may have been available to us, if only we'd Googled one up! Too many well functioning relationships, even cohesive families have been torn apart by such unconscious thinking and action.

Those of us aged over fifty (still young today) have become prime targets for certain advertisers who've decided that, as a 'demographic' group we have disposable incomes. It's been determined that we've paid off our mortgages and lodged our residual meagre savings into a corporate superannuation fund. (The one we were told would set us up for life but has actually dissolved into a pocketful of change through inflation, poor governance, and corporate investor corruption.) The corporate spruikers nevertheless promote the idea that this ripe to target sector, mostly retirees, should take out a 'reverse mortgage', borrowing the equity in our only real asset, which is our shelter from corporate greed, and from potential misery: our homes.

Competitive premiums for funeral insurance should also be a priority, at the top of our bucket list! Oh yes, the cost of dying has apparently escalated so excessively that we now need to pre-pay our funeral. But this opportunistically invented investment 'product' is a matter of deep concern and a cause of much unhappiness for the not so well off elderly, who are made to feel guilty about dying, perhaps leaving the cost of, it's suggested, an expensive event, their funeral, burdening their surviving family.

Prejudiced by our unrealised, subconsciously archived fears, we watch, read, and listen. Often, we're sickened, but always spellbound by the flood of domestic and commercial dishonesty, brutality and obscenity, the violence, immorality and crime so convincingly depicted in television drama productions. We're shocked and traumatised by news reports of drive-by shootings, murders, rapes, burglaries, bank robberies, road deaths, of man made, natural and industrial disasters. Our wide-eyed, open-mouthed digestion of this pile of piffle is only rudely and loudly interrupted by dizzily intoxicating advertisements - the grossly exaggerated claims of corporations - and by the media's own speculative 'Special Reports' about the 'off-field' misconduct of our world leaders, politicians, sports stars, film stars, and the self inflicted drug and alcohol caused deaths of the morally corrupt, while never forgetting to remind us of our other great fear, the disastrous state of the economy!

Notwithstanding all the wonderful events unfolding in the world every day, it's crime, politics, and war that are the entrée, main course, and dessert on the media's menu. In our lethargy, our apathy, our unconscious state, we can't find the energy to switch it off. And so we read, watch and listen, unconsciously, not realising that someone else is deciding what's important to us, how our money should be spent, and what we should be eating, drinking, driving, and wearing: in other words, what we really need, indeed must have in our lives, if we are to be happy.

But are we seriously expected to feel that we're impartially informed or entertained by this distorted mockery of our world and its' events, to absorb it all unfiltered through our bleary eyes and muffled ears, to eat it all up and be happy? Well, no, actually, because those who would seek to give direction to our daily decisions are counting on our unconsciousness, our being never satisfied but remaining ignorant and fearful, so as to keep all of them in business.

Also adding weight to our unhappiness is our own business, our home business: that of keeping abreast of mortgage payments, school fees, energy bills. The fuel and licensing costs for our cars, to get us to and from our place of employment, perhaps some many miles distant from our home, through traffic pollution, congested to the max, depletes our pockets to the last penny. Good gracious! It's stressful just writing this!

So, I see you're still reading, but how are you feeling about all this? Am I painting too dark a picture? Or are you able to see through the smoggy reality, see the sad and horrible truth: a true depiction of our untenable twenty-first-century lives? The same life so many hundreds of millions of people, living in so-called first world, civilized and developed democracies, accept as normal, while at the same time wondering why happiness eludes them.

Understandably, with this diet of personal, environmental, and political calamity delivered into our homes daily *and* nightly, the chance for people to develop a sense of happiness in the world has become increasingly difficult. For far too many, it's become seemingly impossible.

As unhelpful as ever, no politician or anyone in the media will mention the fact that watching that bright screen late at night upsets our natural production of melatonin, the hormone produced in the pineal gland, within our brain, that induces sleep. This causes us to suffer insomnia, sleeplessness, which condition itself contributes further to our loss of energy, of intellectual focus, resulting in poor decision making during waking hours when we should expect to be brightly switched on, not dimmed, dumbed down or completely switched off. To remedy that malady, an unconscious visit to ones' G.P. provides a script for guaranteed sleep and happiness - melatonin in a bottle, the pharmaceutical form.

Of course, none of the aforesaid misery projected by our governments, or advisory and entertainment sources is actually our own misery, and so, few of us are directly affected by it. But we all nevertheless take it on board, because we subconsciously absorb it through every cell in our body. It becomes locked away in our subconscious mind, where it dwells, permanently. And its' subversive, negative effects manifest in our emotions.

Through our natural, human tendency towards identification with and empathy for our fellow people, our brothers and sisters who *are* suffering, we naturally enough identify with the print, television and social media depictions of those less fortunate people's life circumstances, their raw emotions, their wants and their fears, their misery, whether real or contrived by bloggers or news writers, fearing that their dilemmas could so easily have been our fate too. And all the while, unbeknownst to us, that perceived fear and misery is being archived away in our subconscious, where it awaits an opportunity to re-enact that misery in our future lives, when we least expect it, and quite likely to our great detriment.

On the brighter side, you must have heard it said that every cloud has a silver lining. Well, that's true too. Fortunately, despite all the visual and audible misery in the world, we can still be happy, because happiness, contentment, and high self-esteem nevertheless remain our natural state and are our natural right.

The most important thing here is to recognise that in times of unhappiness, our perfectly normal, happy state of being has only been covered up. Our happiness has been misplaced among the layers and layers of our lives' experiences in our subconscious minds' filing cabinet. But happiness is still there within us, it's still available to us, once we learn how to expose and retrieve it.

To have our happiness back, we only need the knowledge and tools to uncover it, to rediscover it, and along with it, reclaim our personal power.

That said, we can only conclude that the answer to this matter of acquisition of a happy solution is indisputable: your self-knowledge and mine, and our own road to happiness through this jungle of greed, misery, and negativity must be surveyed and travelled using our most intelligent means, the means of *conscious awareness*, which dwells within us.

Only as consciously aware individuals can we discover that. We can then navigate our own safe and happy passage through life in our own ways and in our own time. Which, my friend, is what you are doing now. And you must come to know that your only true and reliable guide is your *Self*. Significantly, if we're to attain enduring happiness, we have but little choice in the matter.

The happy paradox here is that this world full of pain and suffering is also full with opportunity for us to learn from our failing or falling, to then alter course, steering our lives in another, better direction.

It's ironic then isn't it, that we humans have seemingly created all the pain in the world for the purpose of bringing us to our ultimate low point, our unhappiest point, where we finally decide that enough is enough. It's here finally, that we find the strength deep within ourselves to embark upon our journey of rediscovery, our road to *Self-knowledge* to *Self-enlightenment*.

Given the many differing circumstances and thousands of events we encounter in a lifetime, it seems inevitable that our life's journey will eventually bring us face-to-face with our ultimate fear, unhappiness. So many millions began this life in a less than happy home or institution where discipline was meted out in a blunt and physical way. Diet was heavily weighted towards sugar-charged fast food and drink. Illicit drugs and cigarettes were considered desirable pleasures, and frighteningly realistic violent computer games were their only entertainment. For the lucky ones, this home-life was overlayed with a school curriculum, which nevertheless demanded academic striving, imposing personal achievement pressure. Even in developed countries, such an environment has been the norm for a very large portion of people in the world, and with such a crucible for life, such a gauge to define or measure their level of happiness, those born post the 1960s would have difficulty differentiating between what is good for them and what is not, what is real in the world and what has been contrived or imagined. Disillusionment about what the world offers in the way of certainty and security is a serious concern for too many. Tens of millions asking; "Where is *my* place in the world". And; "How and where *can* truth and happiness be found"?

In particular, since the advent of television and the Internet, material gain at practically any cost, and violent crime at incalculable cost, have become fully integrated into our way of life. These globally developing, tragedy-strewn environmental plagues, which are the cause of so many peoples' *perceived unhappiness,* have exploded.

In another example of an unnervingly close, yet invisible, cause of unhappiness, most recently, critically informative, although seldom if ever applauded studies, cite strong links between our biology and sociology and crime. It's proven that in the same manner that some of us are born smarter than others, some people are born or delivered through unfavourable early childhood to being predisposed to becoming violent or committing criminal acts. Born predisposed to an unhappy life. This new evidence confirms that our emotional behaviour is both genetically and environmentally influenced. And so, clearly, relying upon the treatment of such a condition with some form of retrospective remedial therapy in a state correctional institution can only be regarded as leaving it too late. It's crucial that self-knowledge and life-management skills, so fundamental and integral to our early learning, be given the highest priority by our governments and our primary educational institutions, if we hope to ever eradicate uncontrolled, unconscionable human behaviour in the future.

Notwithstanding these plainly evident but seldom-discussed causes of people's unhappy life outcomes, the killer punch for many hundreds of millions of us is that much of our unhappiness results from the foremost message of western culture's institutional education, business practice, and lifestyle, which demands that to be happy and successful, we must *strive.*

So striving too, is rampant, becoming a detrimental practice in our modern world, in both the corporate sense and our personal lives. Naturally enough, someone striving to win means someone else is losing, which may mean their suffering disillusionment. And because we're constantly trying to outdo our business and sports competitors, our fellow students, our peers, and our neighbours, we often set ourselves extraordinary, often unachievable goals, causing us to overstretch our financial, physical and psychological capacities. Gosh! It's exhausting stuff!

In this paradoxical twist of fate, our pursuit of happiness has brought about our unhappiness!

The happy paradox here is that this world full of pain and suffering is also ripe with opportunity for us to alter course, to steer our lives in another, better direction.

It's so important to recognize that a perfectly normal happy state-of-being has simply been covered up by the layers and layers of our life experiences.

It's proven that in the same manner that some of us are born smarter than others, some people are born or delivered through unfavourable early childhood, to being predisposed to becoming violent or committing criminal acts.

Chapter 4

Your Unhappiness

Right at this time, as you read this page, only *you* can relate to the form of unhappiness that *you* are experiencing, to the depth of *your* unhappiness, and, importantly, to what or whom *you* consider or have *perceived* as the cause *your* unhappiness. Perhaps it's more correct to say that only *you* have an idea about what particular *expectations you held* that have not been met.

Obviously, these are important matters, but just for now, I'd ask you to set aside any thoughts on that subject. Instead, I'd like you to engage your conscious mind for a moment, to sit still, to be mentally still, and to listen to your heart. Listen to and feel what's there. Because you see, there's something else you didn't previously *know*. Which is that you are not reading this book because you're someone who's thriving on their unhappiness, or revelling in their misery.

Consider this advice to be very good news, because, although like all of us you may well be capable of living in misery, importantly and tellingly you're not comfortable with living in it. The very fact that you're reading this book is a demonstration that you are coming to your awakening, to *Self-enlightenment.* You sense there's a better way. Yes? Of course there is. And your true *Self* is pointing you in the right direction. Otherwise, you'd have stopped reading this book and put it down long before now.

I'm not trying to tease you here. If you are feeling teased or frustrated, it's not my intention. My intention throughout the preceding chapters has been to make you aware of aspects of your world and its' influences upon your life within it, which have been hidden from your *conscious* view, and to shake you out of your old *subconscious* life paradigm—the one that's not working for you, not serving you, the one that's been holding you back, keeping you in need, in doubt, and suffering in unhappiness. I wanted to paint a picture for you illustrating just some of the ways that unhappiness, even misery, can creep into your life unseen. How it can sneakily become an integral part of your paradigm for life, tricking you into *believing* that it rightfully belongs there and that the pictures it paints are of how life is meant to be. Period.

In the chapters ahead, we'll explore new ideas for better dealing with your life and the challenges that life presents you, ways for detecting, even forecasting unhappiness, so that you can always avoid it before it can manifest. There *are* ways to build your life anew, a new paradigm, a blueprint that will serve you, working for you, not against you.

Right now you want to know how to achieve this better way of living because so far all we seem to have done is travel the gravel road of *unhappiness*. While this is largely true, it's been a necessary journey. You see, it's critically important to also understand unhappiness and how it manifests in your life, because, if you are going to win happiness in the battle of life, you'd better get to know and to understand your enemy.

Let's take a break here, to review what you've learned so far.

You've learned about aspects of your life's journey that perhaps you hadn't given consideration to previously.

Since birth, right through into adulthood, for better or for worse, you've developed a subconscious life paradigm; a template created in a part of your mind you never *consciously* knew existed.

You now realise that throughout life you've been unknowingly influenced by that powerful subconscious force, your subconscious mind.

Despite years of education, where fear or the threat of reprimand was used as a deterrent to your failing, you've actually been taught very few life-management skills.

You've acknowledged that today, societies use shallow material values as a measuring stick.

Your eyes and ears have been inundated with horrible news, with stories of wars and famine, civil un-rest, crime and corruption, unreal reality shows, gratuitously violent movies, media hype, and intoxicatingly seductive but exaggerated, and mostly implausible advertising.

You've likely been made empty, unachievable promises by your parents, teachers, peers, and politicians, much of it closely followed by feelings of disappointment and the sufferance of insincere apologies.

It's a fair bet you hadn't considered there'd be so much negativity imbedded in your subconscious, arrived there from every source imaginable, beginning perhaps with the first "No!" from your mother.

You were nevertheless encouraged by the very same sources to pursue a successful life through striving to beat others to the punch, and perhaps borrowing more money than you could afford to repay.

Having this deluge of negativity influencing your life has hardly been a recipe for happiness, has it? But it has surely been one for a feast of emotional adversity. Let me ask you, sincerely, whether there is any chance that this twenty-first-century, material-world formula for life could be working for you, contributing towards the attainment of enduring happiness? No?

Now that you know that throughout your life it's been your unstoppable, preconditioned subconscious thinking that has been your enemy, this new knowledge will enable you to turn that situation around and make your mind your friend.

Now some more good news! (Yes, there's always more good news for those willing to reach for it!) In the coming chapters you'll learn about what happiness really is, just how it *and* unhappiness manifest in your psyche. You will learn how to create an entirely new paradigm for your life, a new map for finding your way forward to enduring happiness. You can rest assured enduring happiness is within your financial means and mental capacity to achieve. It's your right to have, and it's free.

Reaching a new and deeper *Self-understanding* will allow you the freedom to give up striving, to give up thinking and give up the need to know that keeps you caged up in fear, driving you to distraction. Because always having to make excuses, to hide from others, or try to make things right when the events and circumstances in your life seem outside of your control, or when others' behaviour seems threatening or simply at odds with your own, will always deplete your energy, drain your life force, and diminish your personal power.

You can thank your present life crisis, and your perceived unhappiness arising from it, for bringing you to this point. Soon you will leave that perceived unhappiness in your wake, as you move on to true and enduring happiness.

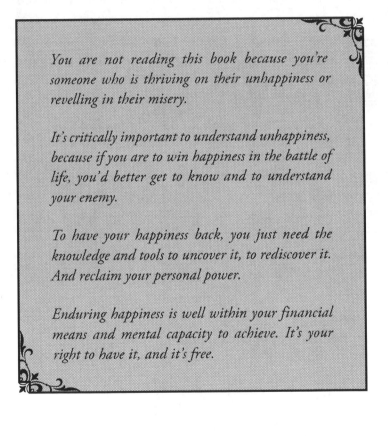

You are not reading this book because you're someone who is thriving on their unhappiness or revelling in their misery.

It's critically important to understand unhappiness, because if you are to win happiness in the battle of life, you'd better get to know and to understand your enemy.

To have your happiness back, you just need the knowledge and tools to uncover it, to rediscover it. And reclaim your personal power.

Enduring happiness is well within your financial means and mental capacity to achieve. It's your right to have it, and it's free.

CHAPTER 5

The Happiness Trap

Given the previously described "multiple whammy" of impediments to a happy life, and without much spiritual depth within our modern society and social culture, it's been through our very striving to get and to achieve, to attain wealth by stealth, by social and corporate ladder climbing, that we have developed a propensity to become strongly attracted and attached to so many of the very situations we ought to have avoided. You might say; "so, we've become trapped, like a monkey with its hand full of tasty nuts in a narrow-topped jar". We have, and like the monkey, we don't want to let go of the prize. But we must.

You see, as if things aren't bad enough, there's an even worse factor to our dilemma, which is that although it's not widely understood why, many of us actually seem to thrive on negative emotions: unhappiness. We actually choose unhappiness! As unlikely as this may seem, through unwittingly surrendering to our subconscious minds, and despite the obvious unhappiness we suffer because of it, we can *think* ourselves into *believing* that we're happy, that we're actually connected to, accepted by, or secure within our relationships with other people and with other things. How can this be? Well, because even a very painful relationship can satisfy our basic human desire and our fundamental need for acceptance, for feeling we are part of a relationship, part of a community, of our society as a whole. And we need that feeling, because it enables us attain a perception of our individual rank or position within our tribe, which in itself brings to us our sense of belonging.

For example, if your childhood home was one where unhappiness, domestic violence, or poverty prevailed, in an unconscious attempt to recreate that environment, without developing conscious awareness, you will subconsciously seek to create a similar or matching environment in which to thrive as an adult.

This seemingly bizarre behaviour can easily be explained. You'll remember that it was our childhood home that was our crucible; it's where our subconscious began to store our experiences, where our life paradigm was formed, whether it was happy or unhappy, stable or unstable, volatile or even violent. In our very formative years, it's what we knew and were satisfied and contented with as a safe and secure home environment. Because we have that archived information in our subconscious, our subconscious accordingly has us tricked into believing that it's in that same environment where we'll be secure and thrive best now, as adults, just as we did as very young children. Accordingly, we unwittingly, subconsciously seek to recreate much the same environment in adulthood. Without ever *consciously* choosing a different environment, we will live with the consequences.

Embracing this notion, we can now quite possibly forecast unhappiness and difficulty in an individuals' future life, or within a relationship, or even predict a relationship's demise, when one partner within it grew up in an abusive or unhappy household.

But no one should feel bad or guilty about ones' upbringing. So many of us were born into or grew up in less-than-ideal homes, where such detrimental circumstances as unemployment or financial concerns may have led to family fears of loss, perhaps to anger and volatility, where parents argued and, if subjected to violence or abused as children themselves, may have acted out of their own fears by abusing each other and their children. There are so many possible events and circumstances that may have contributed to our life paradigm, so many possibilities leading to a subconscious mind full of fears, formed in those most formative years.

With that template for a life and those fears embedded in our subconscious, and without developing an intellectually conscious awareness of our condition, we simply continue to act completely subconsciously, unwittingly making great effort to seek out or recreate the environment of our childhood.

Knowledge about this subject is widely available. It's been derived from years of research, yet it's news to almost everyone, and living in ignorance of it will likely result in a persons' enduring some form of recurring, debilitating unhappiness.

For you and for me, for so many millions, our early childhood experiences, whether happy or abusive, being spoiled or being neglected will have left a biological trail. But our crucible, although strongly built, is not impenetrable, not unbreakable.

We can still choose our own life path. We can *choose* happiness.

Despite all our hopes and wishes, despite our natural desires to live happily, this paradoxical situation endures because it's that childhood environment that fits neatly and comfortably with the secure home life paradigm of the subconscious. It's as if we're reassembling the pieces of a favourite childhood jigsaw puzzle. From our adult point of view, on the surface the finished puzzle looks all right; it just somehow doesn't feel all right. But we don't know why. That's because we've never consciously learned how to put it together any differently, until now.

Equally detrimental to a life of true happiness, we might have been raised in a happy home, one full of joy and laughter, but we may inadvertently have chosen a partner who unbeknown to us was not. Their unconsciously seeking to recreate *their* former unhappy and dysfunctional childhood environment can bring the new relationship undone as we become entangled in the drama that unfolds. Either way, we are likely headed down the road to unhappiness because, in our naked pursuit of recreating the illusion of security, of remaining within the tribe, or striving to keep our act together, we are quite capable of living in what is in fact suppressed old misery. We're living unconsciously, in our unrealised, unresolved unhappiness. In the dark! Which is not actually living at all!

What is so perilous about that is that the perceived feelings of security or happiness that arise from our effort to build a life using the blueprint of our life-paradigm-forming crucible, our unknown and long forgotten unhappy childhood home environment, are in themselves total myths. They're nothing more than a recreation of our subconscious minds' perception. And we have been unconsciously drawn back into them, no matter how wrong for us they might be.

Continuing to live in this way means inevitably that even more layers of subconscious mind perceptions are piling up, burying more deeply our happiness potential. More and more subconscious mind perceptions accrue on top of the original pile, making life ever more difficult to understand. We become blindly entangled, going around in circles from one disaster to another, repeating the same mistakes and getting the same unwanted results from life and relationships. Unhappiness begets unhappiness. Nothing else seems possible. We keep using the same old template for life because we don't know of any other. Hence, we remain unaware and internally blind.

Similarly (now this is really important, so I ask that you please pay particular attention), any sense of unhappiness or insecurity that we derive from these illusions is equally nothing more than our subconscious minds' perception. It's not real, either! Our unhappiness isn't real! And isn't that a huge relief?

You now begin to see what's so incredibly perilous about your subconscious mind. Your perception of its primary use to you is wrong. It's only a storage box, much like an external hard-drive, not programmable but designed to store and recreate your past experiences. So you couldn't call it a good reference point from which to set about creating a life of happiness could you? Because, you don't want your archived, unhappy past recreated do you? So what's the solution? How will you start life anew?

The solution is this: *you must learn to still your subconscious mind, to silence it, if you are to live life from another, more reliable, reference point, from Self-awareness, your intelligent, conscious awareness.*

However, before we move on to that, let's fully understand what has further deepened your unhappiness dilemma. What has in fact invisibly but not indelibly injected unhappiness into your life is the fact that when you unwittingly adopt subconsciously perpetuated perceptions into your life, embracing them wholly, believing them to be real, and living by them, those perceptions or myths, become yours alone. They are not seen or given to any consideration by others in the world. You end up living in a bubble of delusion of your own making.

Living in such false reality we become islands, isolated and exposed on all sides, in a state whereby we can easily and unwittingly increase our emotional fragility. Simultaneously, we exacerbate our other strong propensity, which is that of feeling unaccepted and insecure whenever we feel rejected by or disconnected from others, including rejection or disconnection from our tribe. We're left living at odds with our archived, subconscious perception of what our perfect living environment ought to be.

Being so at odds with our surrounding social world, we can only experience conflict, conflict, conflict.

Can you see how, as a consequence of our lack of conscious awareness, we are vulnerable to becoming dependent upon our perceived connections to others for our security and unable to function effectively as individuals? When we perceive that others have let us down, as so often happens, we are left totally susceptible to becoming disappointed, disillusioned, and emotionally isolated. We're psychologically prone to losing our personal power and along with it, any sense of our true self.

If you're now thinking either, "Gee, life stinks," or "Hey, this is not easy to follow," let's clarify the content of the preceding pages by examining some examples of how emotionally disturbing events in other people's lives might have brought about a perceived sense of unhappiness in them. Or, conversely, see how a perceived sense of happiness and security that was nevertheless equally fragile was wholly responsible for delivering the person into the darkest abyss. You'll discover how without conscious awareness their unhappy life issues could never have been repaired by any further subconscious perceptions such as perceived happiness or perceived re-connectedness. Simply put, you'll see how a second myth cannot counter-act or repair the first myth.

In the following chapters, using your own conscious vigilance, look out for four examples of how unhappiness might manifest in a person's life, indeed perhaps may have manifested in your own life, since your unhappiness may well be the result of some similar event. Whether it was or not does not matter. What matters is that you grasp and fully understand the true nature of your subconscious mind, and the true cause of your own perceived unhappiness. Knowledge is power, empower yourself.

I hope these examples will help you in your understanding of how the complex mechanisms of our minds can and do create a world of mystique and false reality for us. With this new understanding, your Hi-way ahead to happiness, which you'll travel later, will be wider and smoother, no longer potholed, misty or confusing. Life will make complete sense to you, be easy to navigate, and will lead you to the enduring happiness that you desire and deserve.

Example 1: Paying It Forward

We begin by examining the experience that I'm most familiar with: my own. In describing my own life crisis experience in chapter 1, I stated that a full eight years after they dissolved their unhappy marriage and separated, Ron and Penny still found the energy to fight over ownership of a worthless television set and other equally insignificant issues. That they still fought over custody of their children, even custody of a dog. That blinkered by their narrow, stubbornly imbued, subconscious paradigm for life, and without the slightest consideration for the negative impact their wrangling might be having on their children or on relationships with others, completely oblivious to the destructive ripples they created in an otherwise harmonious pool, they acted out their old bad habits in an unconscious attempt to recreate their former unhappy childhood home environments.

Despite these two apparently intelligent adults outwardly projecting a successful and happy picture of themselves to the wider world, the old bad habits embedded in their subconscious in childhood, ruled their inner world, and brought them undone.

It was only later that I learned they both had grown up in unhappy homes, toxically contaminated crucibles for the formation of a life. One had, at an early age, tragically lost a parent in an accident and still lived with the unresolved grief of that event, as well as with the further burden of fear of a bitter, angry, and equally fearful surviving parent. The other had an abusive father, a fearful, war-traumatised, returned solider, who was frequently drunk and would cane his children's legs, sometimes until they bled, and often for little more than minor infringements of family rules. You may or may not be surprised to learn how common these kinds of childhood experiences and family environments are. For some children, home is a war zone.

The great irony and the hidden blessing in my experience was Ron's and Penny's paying their debt forward. You see, whilst Ron and Penny each owed a debt to the other, a huge apology, for past poor behaviour, what transpired, due to their bringing even more drama into their lives, was that they paid that debt forward, on to me.

God (the power within the universe) works in mysterious ways!

The great gift they and the other misery I observed and experienced has given me, has been to bring about my need to discover my own conscious awareness, my Self-realisation!

Through gaining a deeper understanding of my subconscious mind, I was able to let go of my own perceived unhappiness and move on, a happier and wiser person. I'm so grateful for their having entered my life, playing an integral role in bringing about my need to examine the causes of my own repeating of unhappy events, my own reoccurring misery.

In the years that followed, I ascertained that this couple had not only suffered as children but had been abusive towards one another during their marriage. Both were subconsciously addicted to recreating their unhappy childhood home environments, repeatedly replicating in adulthood, what they had been born into. Living ignorant of their condition, they had been unable to overcome their addiction to unhappiness. My hope for them both is that they will find their own state of conscious awareness and use it to create a life of authentic and enduring happiness.

Furthering my experience of coming to consciousness, firstly through directly experiencing my subconscious minds propensity to control my emotions, and then by practising silencing my mind, I have been able shift the power base, back it to its rightful owner, my conscious Self. My own Self enlightenment has demonstrated to me how we can all learn and grow even from our unhappy events, including those brought into our lives by others, that is to say, when others unwittingly bring drama into our lives through their own unconscious actions. Because, when confronted with our fears, we are presented with the great opportunity to turn those fears into knowledge, knowledge about our inner Self, and to grow into conscious awareness.

"But", you will be asking, "just how do we do this"?

The answer is; by doing nothing.

In a later chapter you'll demonstrate to yourself how doing nothing will reveal everything!

To support your understanding of this example, write brief notes here of any similar experience that you can relate to.

....

....

....

....

....

....

....

....

....

....

....

....

....

....

....

....

You might say that we've become trapped, like a monkey with its' hand full of tasty nuts in a narrow topped jar. Like the monkey we don't want to let go the prize. But we must.

The solution is this: We must learn to still our subconscious minds, to silence them if we are to live life from another, more reliable, reference point; conscious awareness.

What matters most is that you grasp and fully understand the true nature of your subconscious mind and the true cause of your own perceived unhappiness.

Knowledge is power. Empower yourself.

Example 2: Bob's Story

In this example, which is an adaptation of a real event, a couple's marriage or relationship ends up on the rocks. One partner—we'll call him Bob—feels particularly miffed. Bob concocts a litany of grievances, directly aimed at his former partner, Betty. His messages to Betty are conveyed with venom, via letters, telephone calls, and texts, accusing her of fault. Bob tells Betty bluntly, in no uncertain terms, that his expectations of the marriage and all it ought to have brought to him have not been met.

Bob's communications may at first appear as though they're designed just to unravel his ex-partner, to get back at her in an endeavour to maintain the upper hand. (Of course, it could easily have been the other way around.) This, despite the fact that the relationship is doomed.

But Bob's crucible, derived from his family history and culture, was one where the man of the house is the king of the house. His wife, however, has no such preconditioning. Throughout their pre-marriage period, Bob's behaviour had been that of a prince, but upon securing his bride, he thought he should be king.

The fact that there's no hope of reconciliation does not deter the complainant, Bob. His subconscious has him on a mission. But what are Bob's messages really projecting? And to what end? Actually, Bob doesn't know what he's projecting. Due to his collapsing marriage being at total odds to his subconscious mind's perception of what state it should be in, he knows only that he's in pain, and he wants relief.

What's really unfolding here is one person's subconscious attempt to dominate another person, and doing it using unconscious behaviour. In Bob's case, that behaviour was not only written and directed by his subconscious but quite likely also employed one of mans primal fears, the fear of loss.

You see, another contributor to our emotions and behaviour, also hidden in the depths of our psyche, are our primal fears, developed over many lifetimes of conditioning—not just recent lifetime conditioning, but the lifetime conditioning of our many forebears, our distant ancestors. It's worth noting here, that aside from your subconscious mind's life paradigm, your genome—your DNA structure—is in fact preloaded, not only with your ancestors' physical attributes, but also with fear and lots of other psychologically embedded elements. But fear is one thing we humans can't live without. It has played a huge role in preserving mankind for tens of thousands of years, keeping us from harm.

Employing his subconscious mind *and* primal fear, Bob was now attempting to preserve what he perceived was his position and security within his collapsing relationship. He hoped to achieve this by effecting and perpetuating a connection with his estranged partner through his flood of written accusations and cross-examinations. But his motivation was always and purely, self-preservation.

Unfortunately for Bob, his messages to Betty manifested in a cold and negative form. This was, of course, wrong, since to achieve the desired result he should have conversed with her warmly and written positively. But he couldn't, because unbeknownst to Bob both his subconscious preconditioning and primeval fear had him in a tight and overprotective grip.

Seemingly cleverly, but actually totally unwittingly (because the subconscious mind is very, very clever at trickery and fooling us into believing that its way is the right way), Bob's every call, letter, text, and e-mail had a predetermined hook entwined in it.

Each message had composed in its' design, the requirement of a response.

Of course, Bob was completely unaware of this, since his subconscious emotional drivers were invisible to him. And it wasn't just losing his partner he feared; far more strongly, he feared losing his subconscious mind's perception of his position in the relationship, and what that position meant to him in terms of its other perception, that of where Bob stood in the pecking order within his wider world. That's where Bob's subconscious perception of himself, his position, and his life environment backfired on him, leaving him lost for truth and love, and vulnerable to misery.

Primal fears are embedded in our subconscious in the same way that our life experiences are, although we no longer need fear being attacked by wild rival tribesmen brandishing spears or sabre tooth tigers brandishing long, sharp fangs! In modern times, due to our aforementioned twenty-first-century values, our fear is more likely of social shame or humiliation, of lost property, lost love, or other social, personal, or financial demise.

Due entirely to his subconscious mind's conditioning—and his genetic composition—Bob believed that the loss of his partner and his position in that relationship would be perceived within society as his own diminished status. He feared he might be stripped of rank within his tribe—never mind stripped of financial and property assets in the family courts.

As mentioned previously, particularly in modern western society, material things have perceived real meaning and perceived real value to us; the loss of them, therefore, is a perceived threat to our personal security. These material values are ingrained in us, infused not only in the individual's subconscious but also in our collective, societal value systems, and so intensely that they have become an integral part of our paradigm for twenty-first-century life.

By now you will have gleaned that due to his genes and his family culture, it's likely Bob's perception of himself was one of having been the king of the household, the stronger one of the two in the partnership, the decision maker, and the one who held the upper hand. Accordingly, to provoke a response from his ex would have given him reason to believe that he was still in control and maintained the higher position in the relationship.

Any reply from Betty would have strangely satisfied Bob, but never for very long, because, of course, he was never actually going to get back what he desperately wanted—quite aside from love and real estate, his subconsciously perceived pride and position. His expressing his accusations and grievances would likely have persisted only until his ex-partner, acting out of her own perception of what the marriage should be, instigated legal proceedings. Then another battle, promising to cost Bob further emotional pain and financial expense, would have ensued.

In an unsympathetic analogy, we might say Bob's behaviour was akin to trying to stay married to someone who'd died. Logically, anyone else can see that there was absolutely no future in the relationship, but due to his subconscious conditioning, the concept of losing his partner (i.e., his assets, his sense of security, and social status) was too frightening to comprehend, and so, in a way, Bob tried to go about life as if his 'dead' partner were still alive, at least as if the relationship was still alive. But in his double-whammy dilemma, his bad behaviour derived from his subconscious perception of his status in the marriage, now punctuated with primal fear (fear from which anger is often derived, as well as other unwanted emotions, like jealousy, volatility, and insecurity), guess what Bob's likely outcome will be. You guessed it! Expensive unhappiness!

In modern western colloquial terms, we might say such a person was living in denial.

It's interesting how we, as a society, full of our own self-importance and purely for reasons of self-preservation, have dreamt up words and phrases to explain away our many undesirable traits. But do you know what? Disease is, and always was dis-ease. A syndrome of the human psyche, an inner anarchy, unrest and turmoil, confusion and disquiet within oneself. What we call illnesses mostly derive from dis-ease. Their manifestation is psychosomatic—emotional or of the mind.

Getting back to our examples, it's very likely that in both examples, Bob's, Ron's, and Penny's subconsciously derived emotional states, and their resulting calamities, are typical of many hundreds of thousands of real cases that have been brought before family law courts. Save for people developing a better, deeper understanding of the subconscious mind and its' power over our thoughts and behaviour, such cases might never reach the courts. Nor would the many tens of thousands of domestic violence incidents resulting from behaviour created from fear and uncontrolled emotions ever occur. The savings in terms of public monies and societal suffering are incalculable. Unfortunately, such deep Self-understanding does not yet prevail. So, much unhappiness in the world results through wide spread ignorance of these critical and fundamental aspects of our psyches, and we endure the suffering, the detrimental impact, that ignorance weighs upon our lives.

In expanding this notion of universally transforming people's Self-understanding in our rapidly socially deteriorating culture, we can envision parents of those millions of unhappy children suffering the lack of presence of a father or mother due to a 'broken marriage', being possessed of better Self understanding. Such enlightenment might see both parents lovingly involved in those children's upbringing and daily lives. Millions of happier crucibles would issue happier adult lives.

To achieve this state of consciousness and Self awareness which *will* lead us to enduring happiness, we must firstly acknowledge our subconscious minds power over us, thereby unearthing and understanding our misperceptions and fears. Only then can we silence the subconscious, extinguishing those misperceptions and the misunderstood emotions and behaviour that emits from them. Through our developing conscious awareness, surely in time, as a people, we must come to learn that unwanted unhappiness, perpetuated by uncontrolled emotional behaviour, is a predictable, treatable, even an avoidable, human condition.

You can begin the process of self-awareness now.

Demonstrate to yourself your understanding of the preceding paragraphs by making brief notes here about examples of uncontrolled behaviour you've observed in yourself or in others that resulted in unhappiness. Writing it down will help you recall and understand that behaviour.

....

....

....

....

....

....

....

....

....

....

....

....

....

....

In summarizing our second example, two aspects of Bob's experience that we must recognize were:

1. That although he didn't know in this very early stage of what could have been his conscious awareness development process—a process that will hopefully but perhaps not inevitably unfold for him over the ensuing weeks, months or years of his life—Bob unknowingly allowed his subconscious mind and the fear within it to direct and control his behaviour.

2. Unfortunately, like many unaware, unconscious people, due entirely to his state of unconscious unawareness, Bob didn't recognise the opportunity to learn, or to grow into conscious awareness, through understanding the truth behind his unfortunate circumstances.

You see, although, like Bob, we can't keep our subconscious from raising the challenges of life every now and then, but we surely can learn to recognise it when it does and shift the weight of power to our conscious Self.

Considering that learning to deal with your emotions has most likely *not* been part of your early home life or your schools' or church's curriculum, without conscious Self-intervention your subconscious mind, like Bob's, could also react impulsively, recalling experiences from the archives of your own distant past to find solutions to present-day events. You can only ever expect that it will bring you the same result as in the past, which is unlikely to be the result you'll want or need, because urgently and unconsciously applying the subconscious mind's same old childhood remedy to a new adult experience usually gets the wrong result. Instead of a partner's or mother's understanding and a comforting hug, it will more likely get a response that could upset, compromise, and possibly even incriminate those involved, in which event your unhappiness and misery will at best continue unresolved. At worst, it will be exacerbated. Neither is a very satisfactory result. You can see that without knowledge of the power of his subconscious mind and without engaging his intelligent conscious mind to remedy his domestic crisis situation, poor old Bob found himself engulfed in a very unfortunate dilemma. He was tricked by his subconscious conditioning into believing that his aggressive, venomous actions would bring back the control, happiness, and security he thought he had formerly enjoyed. He discovered instead that as an adult directing written, verbal, or physical abuse at another, he was never going to be afforded the same level of tolerance, as would a child throwing a tantrum.

Any qualified psychiatrist will tell you that the frontal lobe of the brain, the part that controls, among other functions, our emotional behaviour, doesn't fully develop until age twenty-five or later. For young men it's a longer period of gestation than for young women, and for both it's plenty of time for a subconscious mind to have developed a comprehensive life paradigm, a template or blueprint for its host's future life. Although our Bob may well have been forty-five, what was ingrained in his subconscious shows that being a physically mature adult doesn't mean he's naturally grasped who's in charge of his life.

Acting from subconscious fear, he didn't realise what he was doing. Nor could he comprehend the gravity of the consequences. It was his desperately wanting relief from his emotional pain, from his fear, and his wanting to believe that his messages would bring him some reconnection re-establishing his position and security, that caused him to perpetuate the poorly conceived communications with his partner for as long as he could. His unhappiness, consequently, was perpetuated along with his actions.

You see, you can't help your subconscious from raising the challenges of life every now and then but you surely can learn to recognise it when it does and shift the weight of power to your conscious Self.

In our naked pursuit of recreating the illusion of security, of remaining within the tribe, or striving to keep our act together, we are quite capable of living in what is in fact suppressed old misery.

Despite all our hopes and wishes, our natural desire to live a happy life, this paradoxical situation eventuates because it's that childhood environment that fits neatly and comfortably with the secure home-life paradigm of the subconscious.

CHAPTER 6

Thinking, Believing, and Knowing

Reflecting just a little longer on Bob's unfortunate malady, we might glibly state that this grown man should have known better. That's easy for us to say, but Bob clearly believed in his thinking. He believed that his actions would bring about a different result than the one he got. However, for Bob and for hundreds of millions of people trapped within the influence of their subconscious, thinking, believing, and knowing are concepts that are commonly misunderstood. They're actually all quite different states of understanding. It was, after all, Bob's thoughts and beliefs that got him into trouble. (He'd allowed his subconscious mind to guide him.) And it was his lack of knowing that kept him in trouble. (He had no other, more reliable, reference point from which to take direction.)

Indeed, Bob's thinking had led him to believing, but without Self-awareness, which was absent in his subconscious, it could never have led him to knowing.

Let's more clearly define these often-confused states: thinking, believing, and knowing. Fundamentally, thinking requires you to make effort. Knowing, on the other hand, requires no effort. What does this mean? It means that knowing is a state of awareness that is above and beyond thinking. Knowing just is. It's a part of universal law. Let's use a simple Q & A analogy, to affirm this truth;

Q 1. How do you know that the sun will rise each and every morning?

A. You just know. You don't even have to think about it, it's undisputed.

Q 2. How do you know whether or not the sun will shine through the clouds?

A. You listen to or read the weather forecast. And generally, you believe what you've come to consider are reliable sources, for example, your Internet, local radio, or TV channel's weather forecast. Which, as you know, doesn't necessarily mean it's the truth.

The big question is: Of the two answers above, which answer required effort?

You see, if you think you know, your thinking is your effort. Your pre-programmed mind is engaged and has you under its influence.

Even when you believe you know, again you're making effort, that is, your mind is engaged in recalling what you were told or saw in the past, and again it has you under its influence.

You need to get to *knowing* that you know. Like knowing that the sun will rise. That's where there's no thinking and no believing, no effort required of your mind. It's where your mind, in fact, has no part to play at all. And so no influence over you.

You can see now that your knowing can't start until your thinking stops.

Now imagine living your entire life in this knowing way. Every decision, every choice, every day. Let's call this entirely new state of being without having to think, mind-less-ness.

You'll learn how you can achieve mind-less-ness in a later chapter. You will come to *know* that a true and enduring state of happiness in your life will not result from effort or reading positive affirmations or smiling at yourself in a mirror, which might best be described as narcissism!

Achieving enduring happiness will result from your ability to, effortlessly, make conscious decisions about the directions you take and the choices you make when dealing with the circumstances and events that life presents to you.

As we saw with Bob, when a crisis arises you can always choose to dive in impulsively, blindly trusting the archives of your subconscious mind and, in the darkness there, allow it to manifest a remedy, and you can risk living with the consequences. Or you can intelligently, consciously quiet your mind and, in the deeper understanding that results, achieve an appropriate solution, moving forward in conscious awareness to becoming a better, wiser, and happier person.

There's a certain logic to this don't you think. So this is not that difficult a decision to make. Is it?

In essence, if you are to control your emotions, you must learn about and fully understand from where, why, and how those emotions arose, and what they really comprise. Only then will you see them for what they really are, the manifestation of subconscious thoughts.

Developing conscious awareness will give you back control of your emotions and actions, bringing you to making right choices, avoiding inappropriate actions, and finding happy solutions. If this sounds simple, it's because it is simple, though not so easy to achieve. It will take not effort, but time and patience. But its achievement will surprise and empower you, propelling you outside of and way beyond your current, unconsciously constructed life paradigm, stimulating and expanding your imagination.

Make some brief notes here to record some of your old, and now new, understandings of your own experiences concerning this subject.

....

....

....

....

....

....

....

....

....

....

....

....

....

....

....

....

....

You need to get to knowing that you know. That's where there's no thinking and no believing, no effort. It's where your mind, in fact, has no part to play, and so, no influence over you.

You see now that your knowing can't start until your thinking stops.

Now imagine living your entire life in this knowing way. Every decision, every choice, every day. Let's call this entirely new state of being without having to think, mindlessness. Mind-less-ness.

In essence, if you are to control your emotions, you must learn about and fully understand from where, why, and how those emotions arose, and what they really comprise. Only then will you see them for what they really are, the manifestation of subconscious thoughts.

CHAPTER 7

Moving Forward

Reading thus far, you will have begun to understand that allowing your preconditioned subconscious mind to give direction to your life is sheer folly. Such blindness could eventually lead you, to your horror, to an awful end. The fact is that your subconscious perception of a happy life doesn't necessarily mean your enduring happiness will prevail, or that your life will blend well with that of others or the world. For many people this can be a shocking and quite unexpected discovery and will very quickly escort the unrealised among us to feeling cheated, disillusioned, disenchanted, unloved, misunderstood, and generally without belonging. It can lead to that dreaded state we call unhappiness.

On the other hand, making the *conscious* choice to silence your mind will lead you to developing and utilising *self-awareness*, which supports peace in your life, which in turn promises enduring happiness.

And please, get this:

We must all learn to always intelligently and consciously choose life from this deeper understanding, from our *Self's knowing*. And not by our allowing our subconscious mind control of our engine and steering wheel, the power of impetus and the means of direction we take in life, but rather by consciously engaging our creative minds and natural intelligence, our conscious awareness.

Being able to always make *creative conscious-mind* decisions and choices will confirm to you that like a tsunami early warning system, by your own conscious early detection, the same emotions that have the capacity to lead you into fear and all the unwanted encumbrances that come from that can instead become your ally. Like an instrument being both a barometer and a compass, conscious awareness, will give you a truer sense of your environment and bearing for direction, to maintain a happier course through life. With this greater degree of understanding your newly acquired life paradigm will better fit in with others as well as the world around you. Most importantly, it will help you not to just cope with life's unplanned events but to consciously, intelligently convert them into opportunities for a better life through developing further Self-knowledge. Ultimately, it's only from this place of deep understanding about yourself, from developing Self-awareness, that you'll find your true bearings, your belonging, and enduring happiness.

From this truth, this reality, this most reliable standpoint, you can truly decide your own fate, choosing enduring calm no matter what storms surround you.

After reading this far, perhaps enduring what may well have seemed like having been asked to choose between the comfort and familiarity of your former course in life—your former life paradigm—and a yet unknown but distinctly different life paradigm, and with your previously unknown subconscious revealed and set quietly aside, with your perhaps also previously unknown consciousness awoken, together with new ideas about life to consider, you might have begun to swing your future towards a different, happier destination. That's what I'm hoping for!

And now you deserve to hear some really exciting good news. Conquering your subconscious mind by acquiring Self-realisation and applying conscious awareness, then using these powerful tools to choose your life's path and to acquire enduring happiness, is like learning to ride a bike. Once achieved, it's a skill that will never leave you.

Trust me, conscious awareness will afford you a far more reliable and more peaceful place from which to choose life in future. You'll leave your old, ingrained habits of believing and thinking and live from Self-awareness, from Self-knowledge, from *knowing,* which will be a new, happier state of being and one that will be on tap and available to you always.

In your new Self-realised state, you will experience true peace of mind. (peace *from* mind)

However, for now, make a reality check. You mustn't get ahead of yourself. Until you have this skill and understanding, until you practise *conscious* mind assessment, quieting your subconscious—ultimately achieving mind-less-ness—you and all of us will still have the propensity to be at the mercy of your powerful, preconditioned subconscious mind, which will have you ill at ease about your every challenge, about relationships with others and your world generally, effectively keeping you deprived of your natural, peaceful enjoyment of life.

Without Self-knowledge, your life will hardly be a life; it'll be more life-less-ness, and all due to your subconscious mind's hidden, ingrained fears, your unconscious thinking, and believing, resulting in that familiar sense of helplessness, of always needing to know, whenever life's challenges arise. Needing to know what others think about you, where you personally stand within the bigger picture, within your place in the tribe, within the order of things, and in that dreaded state of wanting. Wanting for things and wanting for love. All of which can only ever keep you caged up in a very tiresome, wearying state of being.

That said, to reaffirm your understanding of what's gone on in your past, let's now reflect on that modern-day measuring stick you used to use.

The new knowledge you're about to acquire will make crystal clear to you something indisputable, which is that acting without engaging conscious awareness and measuring your life unconsciously in material terms, is madness itself. Equally, measuring your own values and sensibilities against those of others is also a huge mistake and will inevitably result in your ending up disenchanted or deluded about the differences that are revealed. Differences that, when viewed from your own individual mind-set, your independent point of view, are going to be diminished, blurred, or magnified. Period.

What will then inevitably happen is that due to your subconscious minds predisposition, to your hitherto hidden and unacknowledged insecurities, you will tend to mentally zoom in on those differences, bringing the small stuff into sharp focus, creating images or perceptions that could then make you feel diminished, believing that others have more than you, or that what they have is better than what you have, and you could begin doubting yourself, your abilities, and your choices.

Conversely, self-flattery being the shortest way to egocentricity, you might puff yourself all the way up to the point of decrying others and, along with that misadventure, diminishing or destroying relationships with your friends, partners, family members or business acquaintances, a result that will impact your life unfavourably. Prejudices, racism, bias, intolerance and bigotry all result from ignorance, from closed or narrow-minded-ness. So, finding a new measuring stick for your sensibilities, values, and your paradigm for living is a venture worth reflecting upon.

You may be thinking at this point; Why do we not understand this stuff, and why would we not naturally do this? It seems a fundamental means to creating a life of harmony within ones self and with others.

Well, as stated in the early chapters, it all goes back to your D.N.A. and to your subconscious preconditioning and of course the fact that it's a contrived and material world we grow up and live in. Another critically adverse aspect to our becoming more enlightened is one that we're all taught from a very early age, both by verbal instruction and through personal physical demonstration by our teachers, parents, and peers, and that is that we must *strive* for a better life, to reach for and achieve the highest position we possibly can. So we strive because striving and comparing our progress against others' seems to be the proper course of action. There ever after at every crossroad, to meet every challenge, from the depths of our subconscious comes the command; "Go hard and strive"! And so we do. Of course striving requires less introspective *Self*-reflection, so it's more in keeping with those other pro-active survival skills we've always been taught, like thinking and mindfulness. And so we more naturally strive, and we measure our performance against others', and we strive further, to better them. This is not to appease only our parents, but also teachers, contemporaries, and, of course, our own perception of our successful self. It's purely ego driven, and because we're not consciously choosing or consciously aware of what we're doing, we are usually bound to suffer the consequences. You may well, right now, be reflecting on some striving you've undertaken in the past that didn't exactly work in your favour.

Trained from an early age in that conditioned methodology for learning, we set out to meet life squarely on, ever striving to reach our own new heights, our own sense of where life ought to take us. Unconsciously unaware of the true source of that ever-elusive thing we call happiness, we subconsciously believe and mindfully expect that our striving will bring to us that other elusive status in life, *success*. As a consequence of our success, in our blind view and *unconscious misunderstanding*, we firmly *believe* that our everlasting happiness will follow......Yeah, right.

What we don't expect, however, is still out of sight. But it's inevitably somewhere ahead of us, possibly just around the next corner. Our greatest lifetime crisis is waiting. Our *Self*-learning is waiting too. It's waiting to show us that our success can be measured in many different ways. In reality, depending upon our point of reference, our perception and our subconscious life paradigm, which has become our measuring stick, the experience that unfolds before us as we move through life, might better be described as un-success. And with the perception of un-success colliding with our subconscious expectations, more often than not, comes our further perception of unhappiness. So following the highs come the lows and about as much fantasy as a fairground ride, a rollercoaster and merry-go-round. Repeated mistake rotations and ups and downs of ecstasy and misery.

Too often the resulting life for many people is one of utter disillusionment. They are surprised, bewildered, even shocked that life has not met with or delivered their delusional expectations. Such reaction is of course just another perception, another subconsciously derived conclusion, as their misery-go-round turns another circle.

Whatever the subject or event, without conscious awareness, all of our "truths" are simply our perceptions arising from our reactions to the many different events and circumstances that life presents to us. For many people, events and circumstances perhaps as ordinary as having a flat tyre or losing a beloved pet or, for a teenager, losing a Facebook 'friend' can result in perceived unhappiness or misery, even depression.

Perhaps for others, it's a spouse of many years in a seemingly happy marriage growing apart from him or her, just becoming old or behaving in some unacceptable way. For too many people, losing money at the racetrack, the betting shop, or the casino is the end of their world, and misery sets in, along with other unwanted consequences. Without conscious awareness, for them, upsetting emotions are not a perception, they are real. Whatever the trigger, for most, the results are likely some degree of some form of perceived unhappiness.

In a much-widened view of people's life experiences, unhappiness might manifest when business partners separate on disagreeable terms or when possession of much desired property is not able to be secured at an auction, or when a family home burns down. Genuine grief is experienced, naturally enough, when a family member is lost through illness or killed in an accident. All these examples are common, everyday life occurrences, and all surely have the propensity to bring even usually emotionally stable people undone, to bring about a state of unhappiness, insecurity, even long-term depression or despair. All these are emotional states or conditions that will likely negatively impact and unexpectedly influence people's lives in some way. Many people don't cope with the fallout. They may collapse emotionally, staying down for a short time or a long time. For some, it can be for a lifetime.

When such difficulties, such happiness-threatening circumstances, arise repeatedly, people might end up measuring their lives by degrees of failure. Yet clearly, it's during these tough times specifically that we need to be able to manage to the best of our abilities and still carry on, happy within ourselves and in control of our lives. But how many of us can? How many of us actually do? How many of us know how?

For people to achieve and maintain better control in their lives, they need a better, deeper understanding about why and how unexpected, unwanted events bring about those unexpected, unwanted subconscious thought processes, which we know now can adversely affect human emotions and behaviour, resulting in fear and anger, tears and unhappiness.

Time to Reflect

I want to pause here briefly to thank you for your perseverance. Although much of what you've read may have seemed somewhat odious and tedious, it will have hopefully helped define for you the reasons for your own perception of unhappiness and given you an insight into the kinds of influences and events that may have brought it about. My big hope at this point is that all these preceding pages will have brought you to new self-reflection, to the prospect of a new and deeper understanding of your psyche, to a new awareness of your powerful subconscious mind's mechanism, and to acknowledging the impact it has had on your decision making and understanding of your position within the world, up until today.

I'm hoping that this new understanding will have brought you fresh views about the world around you, brought enlightenment to your understanding about your true position, controlling the driving force and steering wheel of your life. I hope you take this knowledge with you to achieve your own enduring happiness. Moving forward, you must *know* to wrest control of your life decisions from your subconscious mind, to *consciously* make new and creatively constructed thoughts, which are your means of making conscious decisions, and to not unconsciously allow your subconscious to control your emotions and behaviour. From today onward, it's your conscious intelligence that must take the wheel and steer your life on a better, truer course, the course towards enduring happiness.

I want you to say to yourself aloud: "My life is full of happiness, love, and abundance and was never meant to be difficult. Enduring happiness is my right and my natural state of being."

Don't ever let anyone tell you differently. Those who try to tell you so are speaking from a mind full of conditioning, from their subconscious fears and beliefs, not from conscious awareness or knowing.

Learn in the later pages of this book how to quiet your mind, how to uncover your inner self, which is your true self and your knowing, and how to always live your life from there. Your happiness can only rise and thrive enduringly on that.

List any three things that you do intuitively in life, (perhaps like loving your child or riding a bike) things that you know bring you enduring joy and benefit, and will never leave you.

1. ....

2. ....

3. ....

Now, ask yourself; "How and from where did these arise?"

Conquering your subconscious mind by acquiring and applying self-consciousness and self-awareness and then using these powerful tools to choose your life's path, to acquire enduring happiness is like learning to ride a bike. Once achieved, it's a skill that will never leave you.

Ultimately its only from this place of deep understanding about yourself, about Self awareness and Self-knowledge, that you'll find your true bearings, your belonging and enduring happiness.

Moving forward, you must know to take back control of your life from your subconscious mind, to consciously make new your thoughts, your means of making decisions, and your behaviour.

Tell yourself aloud, "My life is full of happiness, love, and abundance and was never meant to be difficult. Enduring happiness is my right and my natural state of being."

CHAPTER 8

Dispelling the Mystery

To you dear Reader, like many others, *Realization, Self-realization*, and *Self-awareness* are mysterious words and phrases. What on earth do they really mean? You may be wondering what mysterious states of being or depths of understanding, are the gurus speaking about, and how might they relate to you? If I may offer this presumption, you won't realize it yet, but you will later, that *unrealized* was most likely your state of being when you began to read this book. It's suffice to say now, however, based on the fact that you're still reading, it's not a state of being in which you wished to remain.

In your next giant step towards leaving unhappiness and moving onwards to enduring happiness, in a future chapter you'll learn how a simple exercise that you may do at home will lead you from your present state, that of *un-realization*, to a whole new state of being, the one we've been alluding to throughout the past few chapters. I'm referring to mankind's ultimate state of being, *Self-realization*.

And you'll learn to attain that through doing nothing! That is the path to and means for developing and applying conscious-awareness in your life.

You'll begin by gaining an understanding of exactly what reality is. And what perceived reality isn't. You'll do it yourself, at home, by means of what's called conscious recognition, an uncomplicated technique that uses your own personal unhappiness as a case study.

Perhaps now you're thinking, *Okay. I'll learn to attain Self-realization. And then what? What will change for me?*

My friend, everything will change.

But before we move on, so that you'll have a clear understanding about it when you get there, let's talk some more about a phrase I've used a lot so far, this mysterious matter of Self-realization. You may or may not have heard or read much about it before today; either way, let's now dispel some of the mystery that surrounds this subject.

There are many different definitions of the state of being known variously as realized, Self-realized, realization, or Self-realization. You can unearth definitions from an array of different sources. If you wish to study the subject, there are seemingly endless written works on this and other associated subjects, all falling into the self-help and spirituality categories in bookstores around the world. You can download them on the Internet, as e-books. Thousands of Self-realization classes are conducted in pretty much every city in every country in the world, every day. You may choose to attend such a course if you wish. As an introduction to the subject, it will not be detrimental to your quest in the pursuit of inner happiness. Equally useful would be attending an authentic silent retreat. Silence promises to deliver you to an inner knowing state of being, which will also greatly benefit you in your pursuit of happiness.

Most writings on these subjects throw light on, or provide some explanation for, what is so often described as the Self, the inner Self, the true Self, and Self-realization. Wikipedia, an Internet repository of thousands of opinions, quotes for example, the views of many learned people, both the eastern gurus and western psychoanalysts, referring to realisation as; "A profound spiritual awakening, where there is an awakening from the illusory but comprehensibly identifiable self identity images (identities commonly understood to be and described as, the mind, the body and the ego), to the true, divine, perfect condition that in reality, the individual is. i.e. the *Self*"

It quotes; "Awareness plays a key role in achieving Self realization," and "With awareness present, Self-realization should be extremely easy to achieve." As explained by Ramana Maharshi; "Happiness is inherent in man and is not due to external causes" (for example, not due winning the lotto or smiling into a mirror). Accepting this as profound truth, and a powerful insight from one of the great spiritual teachers of the world, you can take it from the wisdom of Maharshi that external causes cannot claim responsibility or credit for your unhappiness either. So, you can begin your change to being happier by not blaming anything or anyone else for your perceived unhappiness!

Wikipedia further quotes: "Even Sigmund Freud, who was initially sceptical of such religious and esoteric understandings, nevertheless adopted them into his theories which have had a lasting influence on western thought and self-understanding. His notion of repressed memories, though based on false assumptions, has become part of western mainstream thinking.

"Freud's ideas were further developed by his students and neo-psycho-analysts. Especially Carl Jung, Erik Erikson, and Winnicott. All have made important contributions in the western understanding of 'The Self', but other alternatives have also been developed. Jung developed the notion of individuation, an assumed lifelong process, in which the centre of psychological life shifts from the ego to the Self."

To compare your own condition, that is to say, how suffering unhappiness has caused you to consider what else life might offer, this is perhaps the best description of the process you're going through right now. I highly recommend that you absorb this notion of Jung's, and to be grateful to have knowledge of it, because few people in the world wake up to truth, making the transition to Self-realization and the possibility of a life of Self-actualization, living life by the direction of the Self.

Perhaps you've already read or heard about some of these many spiritual definitions. Or perhaps not. Either way, you'll understand how some people could become totally confused or skeptical about the subject of Self-realization. To most, it sounds "airy fairy," too steeped in the spirituality culture. But it's only a matter of indifference or irrelevance,

- it's 'like water off a ducks back' - to those who learn nothing through not applying to learn.

I might add here as an example of wide confusion about alternative medicine that even among the so-called professional physicians as a universal professional body, according to Dr Ramesh Manocha, author of the acclaimed work; 'Silence your Mind', there are more than thirty different definitions of the term *meditate*. Consider that statistic for a moment: Thirty different understandings of a practice as widely known and accepted, as meditation. Analyzing just some of these thirty different definitions demonstrates a solid misunderstanding and a large degree of skepticism among the western medical profession about meditation's benefits to mankind. Yet many tens of millions of meditation practitioners wholly disagree with that view. So perhaps it's no wonder that the majority of people of the world are confused about something as seldom taught, as untried and misunderstood as developing *Self-awareness*.

If we bring these two higher-Self-recognition practices together however, we find them to be complementary, that each becomes a means of entry to the other.

Obviously, reading about Self-realization and practicing Self-realization are two very different undertakings. Succinctly defined, one brings a mind full of ideas or concepts, while the other brings a state of nothingness, or to put it another way, no-thing-ness. This means that because the Self is no physical thing, it cannot be described or measured as such. The Self simply is. It is best understood as the life force or energy that you are. Some know it as Spirit or Soul.

The Self is an integral part of you, it is actually *who* you are, that ineffable aspect of your being that is nevertheless reachable and understandable when it is reached. *Self is Knowable.* You can and should always, live by its code and its guidance, which is all-knowing and free from physical-world, mindfully symptomatic restraints.

The constraints of mind, body, and ego are influences that, you will be beginning to understand now, are the same influences contained in your preconditioned subconscious, drawn from your past, from beliefs, experiences, and behavior, all of which has become your life paradigm. These influences would restrain your life's possibilities to those predetermined by your subconscious template, which, to accommodate your life potential, now needs decommissioning, renovating, or replacing.

For the purposes of understanding the matter of your own transition to Self-awareness, consider all of the preceding advice to mean; shifting away from acting and living by genetically inherited, mindfully learned believing and/or by the subconscious mind thinking, to a whole new paradigm, one in which all living is directed and achieved from an inner knowing. Or, when your Self-understanding is more advanced, by the *Self's silent direction.*

Comprehending the subject in this way is, in a way, perhaps less spiritual and, conversely, if your former understanding comes from the psychological end of the spectrum, less psychoanalytical than the terminology more commonly used in spiritualist jargon or in the psychoanalytical and academic phraseology, respectively. You will find that my definition means the same thing, and it's easier to conceptualise for most people.

Similarly, for ease of understanding, your *consciousness* you should consider as your creative mind. Your subconscious mind, however, as you've come to know now, is best described as your habitual, addicted mind. A repository for past experiences, or storage bin!

Next, let's expand your understanding of Self-realisation by stating in the simplest terms, the obvious, something you, by now, already know, which is that your brain has several distinctly different parts, or lobes; that your thinking mind is within one of them, and in your mind is where your thoughts are contained. You're aware that we all have thoughts. What you may not have given much consideration to is this subject of these commonly confused words and terms: thoughts, beliefs, and knowing or awareness, which as we've covered already, are all quite different things.

As described at length in the earlier chapters herein, throughout our lives we've been taught to be mindful and thoughtful, to engage our thinking minds. And also as discussed earlier, the teaching methodologies of our schools, universities, and churches are almost entirely based in learning by memorizing, physically writing or copying from or reading from, prepared texts and scripts that in our first, and critically important, ten or so years of education, are mostly derived from our native country's cultural history, albeit delivered and remembered with a multitude of interpretations. Un-packaging, absorbing and storing this information under the artfully applied whip of fear with which it is delivered, our minds are kept ever busy on this mind-full activity. We seldom question the source or advice of the content and never learn or apply ourselves to do nothing, to actually silence our minds, and allow feeling and inner knowing to guide our lives.

Hopefully, I'm creatively thinking, with the mistiness of mystery surrounding the Psychologists and Gurus terminology now evaporated, you'll be beginning to see where we're heading.

So, for a moment, let's consider this;

When all that we write and say or believe is initiated and/or perpetuated by our thoughts; throughout our lives, we do nothing that we do not first think about. Those thoughts and actions derive from information stored away in our subconscious minds. Consequently, those same thoughts and understandings become our touchstones, then our beliefs. And our beliefs become our life paradigms, which become our actions, no matter how wrong or inappropriate for us, or how well they serve us. Growing up unconsciously unaware is not a crime, but we are much better served by consciously discovering and acknowledging this human weakness and taking action to overcome it, to bring about the life we'd prefer to have, a life of enduring happiness. Yes?

Now, let us move on to the crux of this crucial, richer and happier-life-forming matter. It's time for you to learn to stop all that uncontrolled, subconscious, habitual thinking and then to develop control of your future creative conscious thinking, by developing this state called Self-awareness.

In the state of Self-awareness, you *will* uncover within your being a deep and conscious awareness that; *you are not your body or any part of your mind or your ego.* You may regard them from now on as purely auxiliary or supporting aspects of your being human, realising that they do not dictate the direction of your life. Not unless you allow them to, which, you will have gleaned by now, you must not!

Let's reiterate some of the content of the early chapters here, to make it fresh in your consciousness.

We humans always have a head full of thoughts. And in our usual *unconscious* state, we have the strong propensity to become habitually *attached* to those thoughts, believing them to be real. So much so that they don't willingly allow us to differentiate between reality and unreality, in particular, in stressful situations. Accordingly, we very largely rely on, believe in, and act from, what has been programmed into our subconscious minds throughout our lives, that is, our *preconditioning.* The danger here is that the thoughts that do arise, *arise from our subconscious minds' preconditioning,* and we are consequently always at the mercy of its rigidity, its inflexibility, and its lack of creativity.

Because, never having stilled or silenced our mind long enough to differentiate between the two, we can and do experience painful conflict when our *subconscious minds' recollection* of a past experience, doesn't agree equally with the *reality of a present experience.* The mental expression and imagery that emerges from this conflict, causes us emotional stress and suffering, which, as discussed at length in the preceding pages, soon brings us to the state of unhappiness.

Unhappiness results because conscious awareness is missing.

"Aha!" I hear you say, "So, will this conscious awareness help bring about enduring happiness?" Yes, it will.

Although this process of your gaining a new understanding of the subconscious, of placing a different perspective upon the mind, the body, the ego, and all that we are and what reality really is, makes this a mind-numbing read, there's no substitute for a truly thorough understanding of a subject if you are to "get it", and to reap the benefits, which are truly incalculable, invaluable, and profoundly enlightening.

In writing this work I'm acutely aware that whilst many people prefer one-stop shopping, the fast means to achieving enduring happiness (as well as every other human desire!) reaching a complete understanding of the human psyche requires some degree of *conscious* application. Some aspects of the subject can seem complex, are complex, and are quite new to many; therefore, at least initially, they can be difficult to grasp. Not everyone "gets it" at the same time. You need to be patient. You have to comprehend that there's a process involved. And while you persevere, to attain new understandings you must also be prepared to let go of all that you previously *believed* living your life was all about, to dismantle then reassemble your old life paradigm. All these are humanly do-able tasks, and all worthwhile.

As I'm sure I mentioned previously, it's not easy to give up something that's been an integral part of you, all your life. Your whole life paradigm is rooted in your psyche, in your subconscious mind, which *is* strong, stubborn, and inflexible. It won't want to allow you to proceed.

That's why you must by-pass it!

That's the golden key to your happiness. And so, you will soon see, it's not a matter of climbing this mountain of a challenge, rock by rock or by mirror gazing, by reading sticky notes with written affirmations, nor conducting strange rituals. But it is a matter of taking one single step, the one single step to Self-awareness.

Now lets get to the essence, to some hard-hitting truths.

To understand what it will take for you to achieve enduring happiness, the most important thing for you to do is; to get around to getting it, no matter how long it takes. The lifelong benefits are worth your attention, worth spending the time it will take and having the patience and the courage to substitute your lifetime habitual thinking for silent Self-reflection and conscious awareness. Too bad it wasn't a part of your early education!

To say that you can't because your old habits are impossible to break or because it's too hard is pure laziness, of apathy and ignorance. You can of course choose to remain where you are, as you are, the perfect emotional and psychological reflection of your parents, your ancestors, and to endure all that they endured. Or you can consciously change your habitual subconsciously controlled thinking and consequently your existing life and level of happiness, by learning to achieve, practice and apply, conscious awareness.

So, to discover conscious awareness is your first new goal. This goal will not be achieved or found in any book, any mirror, anyone else's eyes nor any type of thinking or with any type of effort. As stated previously, you will achieve it by doing nothing.

More about that later.....

As explained by Ramana Maharshi, "*Happiness is inherent in man and is not due to external causes. (Neither is unhappiness.)*

Awareness plays a key role in achieving self-realisation. With awareness present, Self-realisation should be extremely easy to achieve.

Your whole life paradigm is rooted in your psyche, in your subconscious mind, which is strong, stubborn and inflexible. It won't want to allow you to proceed. That's why you must by-pass it!

To understand what it will take for you to achieve enduring happiness, the most important thing for you to do is; to get around to getting it, no matter how long it takes.

Let's return now to the subconscious mind and to un-awareness, as we consider another analogy, another example of the type of trickery the subconscious mind might have duped you with.

Example 3. Scary moments at the movies

You must surely have been to the movies to watch a crime thriller, a horror movie or a tear jerker feature, so you'll most likely have observed other moviegoers there, and noticed that whilst the film is supposed to be entertainment, their behaviour demonstrates that it can be a stressful experience for some people. That their emotional reaction to events on the screen or in the script can often take them by surprise. The resulting outbursts of laughter, screams, tears, squeals, or hoots are entertainment themselves. Or not. Perhaps you've experienced these types of reactions being unleashed from within yourself. They might have made you feel foolish afterwards, perhaps even a little embarrassed or self-conscious. You needn't be; it's a very common reaction.

The reason for your outbursts is simply that *subconsciously* you've related or connected the fictitious event in the film to some past experience, either your own or one you've learned about, an image embedded, unseen, and long forgotten, in your subconscious mind. When a similar or comparable event was presented to your eyes and ears on the silver screen, your subconscious instantly retrieved the earlier one; made a spontaneous judgment, a decision to *believe* in the event you were seeing on the screen; and gave you cause and justification to react in the way that you did, in the same manner you did when the original event occurred in your earlier life. For a moment, for your subconscious, the event on screen was real. You see, your subconscious doesn't know the difference between reality and fiction or fabrication. To the subconscious, all similar events carry the same value, and today's special effects are certainly very convincing, aren't they?

Perhaps the saddest aspect of our growing up is that we lose our childhood happiness, our innocence and fearlessness, very early in life. This happy state is quickly overshadowed by our physical world and our life experiences, in particular by our own individual understanding or sense of them. As very young children, we soon establish what's emotionally acceptable and safe and what's not, what we shouldn't be concerned about and what we should be fearful of. These decisions, made during these formative years contribute to both the foundations and the building blocks of our life paradigm, which we unconsciously consider will be our safe and happy future. Todays prevalence of street violence, which is a serious social issue, is considered by some experts to be due to the fact that too many young minds have been subjected to too much gratuitous violence, murder and mayhem depicted in realistic computer games and in movies, to the extent that their subconscious minds are archiving the experiences as 'normal'. To have large numbers of offenders recreating these events in the real world has clearly become a serious threat to security in our society today, and for our future.

That said, it's evident that when very young children, who've not yet subjected to such things as murder and mayhem, are not quite sure how to take us when we make faces or play tricks on them, it is because they haven't yet categorised our behaviour. Nevertheless, their subconscious minds *are* filing the information away, although it's too early for them to decide whether or not ours is safe or threatening behaviour. Time, and further experiences will tell them which is which. Not yet afraid, because no harm has come to them from any such event, toddlers give us the benefit of the doubt, for a time at least, simply turning away, squealing with delight. If you have one or two-year-old toddlers in your household, you'll have observed them behaving in this manner.

Notwithstanding our understanding of a child's subconscious activity, the seeds of that propensity for creating a sense of fear were already sown into your genes when you were born. These are your primal fears, inborn from many generations before you, from your evolution. Without your reaching conscious-awareness, intelligent Self-determination towards some other understanding, that initial state of fear will evolve exponentially, eventually developing to a greater or lesser degree, as your life experiences unfold.

Due to their particular life experiences and living environment, some people may become more fearful, some more fearless. Some become adaptable, some become rigid. Some like you some like me. But all human psychological states are born in the brain, lodged in the subconscious mind. Fear is just one of them, but it's a dangerous one, because, as politician's, the ad men and the media know, fear is the one that most acutely affects, and amplifies our emotions.

Our example above of emotional reaction to the activity in a film is an excellent demonstration of just how subtly hidden and yet how powerful our subconscious minds are. How else could film directors trick us into believing that what is most often highly implausible fiction, is real? Of course we walk from the theatre out into the street, where the power of the imagery in the film is quickly dissipated, but it's replaced by another false reality, that of our twenty-first-century living environment. Notwithstanding the apparent danger inside the theatre, our conscious Self never feels the effects of a creepy movie, and we usually make our way home relatively unaffected.

For some, the more intense images from the movie may have become embedded in the subconscious, reoccurring as dreams. But, as you will by now realise, dreams are just another form of subconscious mind activity. Your subconscious mind soaks up *all* your life experiences, *all* the sounds and imagery, *indiscriminately*, including your reactions, and stores it *all* away, until some future event causes its retrieval. Then, one day, in the midst of a crisis, it surprises you with its revivification and discharge in a completely inappropriate reaction.

You might compare your subconscious mind to a handgun inside your head, one that self-loads and fires indiscriminately! Imagine that, and how much you'd want to gain control of it!

Understanding this subconscious mind storage-and-retrieval process means you can easily justify your emotional reactions to events, labelling them as just that and passing them off simply as memories of things you experienced or mental derivatives of events you saw or heard about at some point in your life in the past. Having this *knowing* that they were simply events that were stored and retrieved in your mind, a lot like images stored in a computer photo file, dissolves them all into proper perspective.

But the ability to make instantaneous assessments of your subconscious reaction to events, and doing it effectively, requires your developing conscious awareness. Because, there's a startling difference when a life-threatening experience, similar to one we might have seen on a movie screen, actually happens in your personal life. Without *conscious awareness*, its impact on your mind and the resulting emotions can be far more profound, and far longer lasting.

Conversely, thanks to conscious awareness, the extent, depth, and longevity of that impact and its effect on your emotions, will no longer be determined by your subconscious mind's recollections of a similar previous experience. It will instead be determined by your conscious recognition of the reality, the true nature of the event, in the moment. Although you may nevertheless suffer a momentary emotional reaction to some degree, what will have greatly diminished that emotional impact is your *awareness*—your Self's recognition and knowing exactly what your emotional reaction was, how it emerged, and how to deal with it and move on in life much less affected. Even, unaffected.

Accordingly, no emotional pain (unhappiness), will arise. Your ship remains steadily on course.

In listing these life experiences, you can include all those ordinary everyday events described previously, such as lost loves, lost pets, marriage issues, money shortage issues, business partners or employees misappropriating funds, cyber-bullying, failing at school or your grandparents passing away, and the many other everyday events that get your mind and head (and arms and legs) into gear—the wrong gear.

By learning to quiet your ever-busy mind, you will learn to differentiate your preconditioned subconscious mind from your *conscious Self* and immediately recognise what's happening in any, perceived to be, threatening situation. A new inner understanding will arise about why your mind reacted impulsively in that instant. This differentiation allows the *Self* to determine *consciously* considered and more appropriate solutions than can your preconditioned subconscious mind. The event and its potential effect on your life and emotions will be brought to an end very quickly.

Your Self's state, which is mind-less, but omnipotent, will overcome and defeat the mind-full-ness of your subconscious, quelling any possibility of inappropriate emotional upheaval, allowing calmness to prevail. All in all, a far better outcome and a much safer place from which to live, yes?

Very few of us can actually remember the very early events of our lives, say before age 3 or 4, but throughout the many stages of our growing up, we will all have encountered, for example, life experiences that resulted in feeling degrees of anger, jealousy and fearfulness. We especially noticed these emotions arise in us in our close or personal relationships, such as those within the schoolyard or the workplace, or when interacting with friends, lovers, siblings, and spouses. This is understandable. After all, weren't these the very people who were most routinely in our daily lives and therefore most likely to have given us lots of opportunities to think about them and to react to them and to particular events? A perceived threat may have lay simply in words harshly spoken, an implied or verbal threat or criticism made that seemed unfair, unjust, untruthful, and generally unlike our own formed views about what should be, not akin to our own sensibilities, our life paradigm, our own truth. Perhaps we suffered physical abuse, the consequences of which have left long-time emotional scars, embedded in our memory.

At times the actions and words of others, whilst not necessarily or deliberately intended to be, *can* seem threatening, not just to our beliefs but to all aspects of our lives, including our relationships, our employment and financial status, to our way of life as we would wish and expect all things to be.

It's during these times especially that our subconscious minds engage in what is clearly irrationality, and our uncontrolled emotions rise to the fore. At the peak of the emotions we suffer, we naturally enough feel at our most fragile, most vulnerable. Accordingly, it's these same times when we are most likely to dive blindly into defensive reaction prescribed by and directed from our preconditioned subconscious. In our ignorance of the deep dark well of archived thoughts and emotions from which our reactive behaviour is drawn, we *unconsciously* desperately hope that our reaction will offset or prevent the act of intimidation or loss or fearful threat that we are experiencing, the fear of or sensing, that we are about to suffer.

You understand this now, I suspect, and you might justifiably ask, "Why, then, do we not tend to immediately recall our joyful, happy experiences? Is my 'well of experiences' full only of fear and badness?"

Actually, no, of course it's not. Your subconscious has *all* your past experiences stored away, not just the bad ones, and you will recall yourself singing along, whistling, dancing, or jumping for joy when seeing, hearing, or recalling fun events such as the sight and sound of a child laughing, a humorous event or listening to your favourite song on the radio, quiet possibly many years after you first heard it. So those happy thoughts will always deliver back to you, happy emotions!

It's well documented by psychiatrists and psychologists that all that we humans do in our life, all our thoughts and resulting behaviours, are rooted in one of only two primeval places within the psyche: either unconditional love or fear. Both of these are indelibly infused into the subconscious mind, from where all emotional reactions to experiences arise.

Consider this fact: Almost all our human emotion derives from; 1. Our unconditional love. 2. Our fears.

This isn't too difficult to comprehend. Even when you consider all the possibilities we're confronted with throughout our lives, if there were just two big bins into which we could place our every personal experience, simplistically we'd consign them to one of these two basic categories.

Consider these points.

1. If we feel love unconditional love for them we will not be threatened or afraid of them. Our likely emotional reaction will be: happiness.
2. If we fear them, we will feel threatened by and afraid of them. Our likely emotional reaction will be: unhappiness.

Thus, as you see, matters of unconditional love don't trouble us at all. *It's only when we impose conditions on love that we suffer, and often from the fear of the loss of that love.*

However, if it's conditional love, it's not real. We have manufactured or contrived it in our minds to seem like real love. *We've contrived it because we were in need of it. But it was a myth of our own making.*

To test this notion: consider for a moment the sense of love you feel for your own children, your siblings, your parents, spouse, or perhaps a newborn child. Feeling un-troubled? Of course you are, because generally that's love of the purest kind. It's unconditional love, love without conditions imposed, without expectations or neediness. Even when they're bad, you love them! It's not an easily accepted notion, but some mothers of murderers have said that they love and forgive their children for their unconscionable behavior. Forgiving them might not save them from the fate of their sentencing, but perhaps a mothers' unconditional love does save them from spiritual obscurity. Those who cannot feel unconditional love for those so related to them are surely troubled souls, born with troubled DNA, with difficult and unhappy beginnings in life, a life cast in a toxic crucible.

Now, consider how you'd feel in your heart if you were physically assaulted, cheated on, were stolen from, sacked from your job, robbed, mugged, or caught in a tidal rip. And how about if your spouse or child or mother or father were injured or killed, your car stolen or damaged, or your home broken into, or if a gun were pointed at you or you were subscripted into military service and sent into war. "Not good" will suffice for an answer. But "fearful" is more accurate. And how would a person feel about someone he or she married solely for money or for social position? "In morbid fear and grave danger of losing them" will suffice in this case.

For some, fear may arise from an event as simple as their parent, child or girlfriend moving to another town, because they have imposed conditions on the love they believe they hold for them, and that love may be lost or not be reciprocated. Indeed the loved person may not even be aware of the invented feelings. This is a very common conundrum for people and is the source of much disillusionment and unhappiness. The perceived fear of loss of the invented love gives rise to other related emotions, such as jealousy, anger, and anxiety. As you can see, it's the events and experiences that we perceive as in some way threatening to our subconscious perception of our wellbeing that trouble our minds the most. Understandably, it's these experiences that generate our more intense emotional reactions.

It's especially ironic, then, isn't it, that it's through these same intensely troubling experiences that mankind has been able to unearth self-knowledge and gain traction in controlling subconscious thoughts and emotions. It was directly from our experiencing fear that we've learned about the source of our emotions. Accordingly, we can learn also to control our fear and maintain our emotional equilibrium.

If, as a species, we had remained ecstatically happy all the time, we would never have had the need to explore our psyche and uncover our most debilitating emotional condition! So it's been the ebb and flow, the yin and yang, if you like, of our lives that comprised the range of ingredients we needed for our spiritual growth, and is what stirs within us our capacity to uncover, to rediscover our Self-awareness, our happiness and contentment.

Since evolving from cave dwelling some ten thousand years ago, we've lost a large degree of our instinctive defense mechanism. Whenever life-paradigm-threatening events arise in the present day, our being utterly unprepared for them has us taken completely by surprise. That is to say, unless we're trained in a military force to be 'prepared for the worst' like soldiers, modern lifestyles have not usually taught us how to cope when under stress. So of course we're equally unprepared to cope with our often over-reactive behavior, brought on by the powerful emotions that quite unexpectedly arise in us.

In such circumstances our most common reactions to threatening events are to;

- Run for cover. For those of us who are best described as non-confrontational, this is a very common and instinctive reaction.
- React defensively. Remember that defensive reaction in some might manifest as harshly spoken or abusively written words (remember Bob) but also that that abuse might be physical, violent, even life-threatening.

Without knowing which type our reaction may be, confronted with certain real events we do nevertheless react and afterwards surely do suffer the consequences, which, unlike the feelings of foolishness after a tear-jerker movie, are more likely to be a hard, blunt blow, the equal of the physical or verbal assault, the abuse or intrusion that we've just experienced. And our residual emotional feelings are far more likely to be profound, usually fear, guilt, embarrassment, and remorse, but possibly worse. Both the abuse and our reaction become part of our life experience and are indelibly recorded in the subconscious.

Without conscious awareness, those who, like you, are on the road to acquiring awareness but not yet quite there are left reeling, feeling isolated, lost, and alone in their thoughts, wondering; *Why and how did this happen? Why am I feeling like this, and how could I have dealt with the event better or more effectively?*

And; *How can I stop this pain and stop it from happening again?*

Collectively; *Why am I so emotionally upset by this event and left feeling in such a state of helplessness and unhappiness?*

And quite possibly; *Why has this unfortunate event happened to me again?*

I know this to be true. It was my experience too.

The good news is that those unhappy events you've experienced in your life brought you to this crucial point whereby you have become consciously aware that your life is not unfolding in a way that sits comfortably with you. You desire change for the better and you're making intelligent enquiry.

As we've said previously, in the absence of conscious awareness, when we find ourselves caught up in unhappy predicaments, our reactions often come as a complete surprise to us. And unfortunately, just like me in my earlier unconsciously lived life, most people fear discussing their unhappiness or their behavioral reactions with anyone else. As a consequence, their life-debilitating emotional pain and suffering persists. By enquiring, leading to your becoming Self–aware, you will transcend the need to talk to anyone about your unhappiness. You will instead radiate a quiet contentment, which will puzzle many of those who knew only your former, unconscious self.

But first a warning. As we become cognizant of the possibility of a higher spiritual state, we must recognize and acknowledge our past limitations. Because without having yet developed the ability to control our subconscious thoughts and reactions, it's in the midst of those happiness-threatening situations that we can still so easily, inadvertently and unconsciously, allow our subconscious minds to rule, even to run riot.

Making some brief notes here, in your own words, will help you recall situations or experiences that you relate to this subject.

....

....

....

....

....

....

....

....

....

....

....

....

....

....

....

....

Our Self's state, which is mind-less will overcome and defeat the mind-full-ness of the subconscious, quelling any possibility of inappropriate emotional upheaval, so allowing calmness to prevail. A far better outcome and a much safer place from which to live.

You see, your subconscious doesn't know the difference between reality and fiction or fabrication.

You might compare your subconscious mind to a hand gun that self loads and fires, indiscriminately! Imagine that and how much you'd want to gain control of it!

If, as a species, we had remained ecstatically happy all the time, we would never have had the need to explore our psyches, to reveal our most debilitating emotional conditions! So it's been the yin and yang, if you like, of our lives that comprised the range of ingredients we needed for our spiritual growth, and is what stirs within us our capacity to uncover, to rediscover our Self awareness, our happiness and contentment.

Example 4. Jumping to conclusions.

In this example, a personal life crisis unfolds when a young person's subconscious gives rise to her perception of unacceptable behaviour in a friend. The result is her perceived unhappiness. Engage your conscious mind as you read and imagine the following events;

A young student recently met a new love. She borrowed her new boyfriend's computer and inadvertently or perhaps mischievously opened a file, discovering what she perceives to be photographs of his ex-girlfriend. Due to our young student's past experience of losing a former boyfriend, which resulted in her feeling insecure about the possibility of another boyfriend having another girlfriend, her resulting urgent need to erase this possibility - which is causing her a high degree of emotional discomfort - from her mind, prompts her to quiz her boyfriend harshly, levelling unwarranted, irrational, personal questions at him about his former friendships.

Regardless of his answers, her subconscious preconditioning causes her to think and feel, *He's still seeing her, going out with her. Maybe he's sleeping with her!* With her mind now running wild, her thoughts escalate. *She's getting all his attention, and I'm not!* Then ultimately: *He's going to dump me for another girl!*

The emotional reaction unfolding for our young student we'll call 'jumping to conclusions', conclusions that have manifested, then erupted, from her subconscious recollection of some past experience, an experience filed away in the storage bin of fear that has her held in the grip of fear of loss of love, and of threat to her security. For her, the fear of such an event reoccurring may have been derived from her own emotionally painful loss or possibly from someone else's loss, perhaps her mother's loss of her father's love, or some similar event, perhaps even having lost a much-loved family pet. Loss of love can be experienced in many forms.

When faced with a similar threatening situation, no matter that it's purely fabricated in our subject's mind, those old, unresolved emotions based in fear of loss are instantly manifested in her mind, and they begin to swell inside her, bringing about anxiety and resulting in an unhappy state.

As she continues to think about it, repeating the thought processes in her mind, her belief becomes further and further embellished. Her imagining the story she has created in her thoughts becomes more and more intense, more real. So real in fact, that eventually she believes that the subject of her thoughts *is* real, *is* the truth. Of course, it's not, but for her, in the state she's in, it has come to be, so for all intents and purposes, it is. It has become her reality. She doesn't realise it, but it's now her own invented reality, her own "truth." *Despite her having made it all up in her mind, where her out of her control, powerful, preconditioned subconscious recalled it from the past, or reinvented it.*

Her resulting suffering isn't real, either. It's just another perception. But without conscious awareness, the sufferer's imagined story seems real, and for her, the distress also seems real.

You can see that it wouldn't be difficult to imagine a different example of jumping to conclusions where, let's say, a businessman has discovered irregularities in the company's books and accuses his accountant of cheating, of stealing the money. The accountant's denying any wrongdoing is not convincing enough to dispel the fear burning in his boss's brain. The boss screams accusations and, in an uncontrolled fit of bad temper, pulls a gun from his office drawer and fires. This is the stuff of many television crime shows. But is all of it invented?

Whatever the circumstance, the same kind of reaction could result whenever the thought is one that is driven by fear. In the earlier example, it is a very strong and primal fear, the fear of the loss of love. And, of course, a teenage girl also fears the loss of all the benefits that might come with his being her boyfriend, with her perception of her social status on campus, when being seen by her peers proudly walking with him after school.

In the second story, the businessman fears loss of money, loss of his business's revenue and all that would result from that: inability to make the payroll or meet the monthly overhead, or having his clients, his competitors, and the media learn about his weaknesses or business practices. He fears that not making his mortgage payment could lead to his marriage and family breaking up. The list of possibilities is endless. In the past he learned about and stored away in his subconscious knowledge that these things do happen, that many a business has been brought down in this way. On top of this, he's already suffering the stress of running a small business on a tight budget, which can be stressful in the extreme; stressful enough to resurrect a plethora of subconsciously archived and unresolved fears.

People have actually been shot dead by their clients and business partners for wrongdoing, for giving bad advice or embezzlement of company funds, an event in itself reason enough for some degree of fear. And discovering the truth about an innocent bookkeeping mistake, after the event, when there's no hope of resurrection for the deceased victim, is cold comfort for all involved. The mindfully out-of-control innocent boss's subconscious begins to picture him landed in jail, and the full extent of damage destroying his family, which image completes this sorry picture.

The facts are that without our engaging conscious awareness, our subconscious can be the source of great distress and our absolute undoing. Of course these last two are fictitious examples; however, the irrational thoughts that arise in the preconditioned subconscious mind when such circumstances occur can instantly become equally deeply embedded irrational beliefs. The result could be a form of paranoia, which might best be described as a strongly held *perception* in the subconscious mind which is false reality, and quite different from, and outside of, what we'd call normal thought processes, is not just a momentary state. Due to fear from the perceived threat they impose, subconsciously stored thoughts can and do explode beyond the thinker's capacity to control them, and the mind can remain in that state for a long time. Quite possibly for a lifetime, since without intelligent, conscious awareness, where Self-intervention brings a deeper understanding about the processes that have occurred in the mind, the thinker completely loses all sense of reality, all rationality. The result is that some people do imagine, say, and do, very irrational things. These are things we're all capable of doing or believing, to some degree, when conscious awareness is absent. Our unaware young student became completely stuck in her thinking and could not un-think those thoughts, causing her paranoia and inviting a serious state of unhappiness to set in.

Let's imagine then, what other events might have unfolded for this hapless victim of her subconscious.

Upon discovering the photographs, our student sends twenty confrontational text messages to her boyfriend and makes ten irrational telephone calls to the supposed ex-girlfriend, in the middle of the night! In desperation she discloses her suspicions to someone who she thought might soothe her pain but who actually takes advantage of her plight and humiliates her in front of fellow students. Days, even weeks later, when her mind won't stop churning and the fire in her head won't stop burning, she can no longer sleep. Like a revolving door, *the thought processes, the suffering and the emotional reactions continues to revolve, around and around.* Wretchedness becomes her new reality; a state of emotional darkness prevails. Unrealized, debilitating unhappiness sets in. Her studies begin to suffer, and she drops out ... or worse.

And the businessman ... it's perhaps too frightening to imagine what might have unfolded for this fellow, so let's not explore his story further, lest we too become entrapped in the illusion!

Though some are invented, all these preceding examples illustrate how unhappiness can creep into one's life through uncontrolled, irrational behavior derived from subconscious thoughts, and from over-thinking. And they are not so uncommon. They could easily be real events in people's lives.

You may have personally observed situations where people have become emotionally distressed, even fearful, when a family member or friend is late for dinner, when a jet airliner has hit turbulence, when children have failed to call home while sleeping over at a friend's place. For those involved, who's past experiences are triggered by the thought that something may be amiss; the prospect of harm or of loss of a loved one can be a frightening event for some people who might become frozen in fear, their lives turned upside down. Besides those we've explored, road accidents, house fires, even lost jobs, especially those when close friends, or valued possessions are lost are all common events that could potentially emotionally upset us.

If only all people possessed Self-awareness, a deeper understanding of their human psyches, and could differentiate between perceived reality and reality, and instantly find inner peace, then perhaps their fears and emotional suffering would quickly abate, and their lives remain steadily on course.

Whenever such frightening situations arise, your first conscious step to gaining control is to quickly, consciously recognize what is real and acknowledge that if your emotional reaction is one of fear, you are possibly over-thinking the matter, that your subconscious mind has become engaged. The next conscious step is to not allow your subconscious to establish the story, nor embellish the story, especially to the point that it seems a threatening "reality."

An out-of-control state of mind and all the attached emotional pain can establish itself and stay with you for months. For the unrealised it could stay for a lifetime, its dark presence thwarts their ability to live natural, carefree, happy lives. In severe cases they may become detached from friends and society, perhaps even seriously introverted and distrusting, and may find great difficulty in maintaining relationships or forming new ones. As a consequence, their interpersonal skills never develop. Lost in the darkness that prevails, a greater number than you could ever imagine actually choose suicide. For most of us, however, the result is some degree of disappointment, disillusionment, or unhappiness.

Being stuck in this pattern of thoughts and resulting pain could perhaps best described as an *habitual state of misery*. Call it what you like, it's a dark and awful place to find yourself. And in the depths of your suffering, there seems no way out.

But there is a way out. A portal to truth and reality can appear when you'd least expect it to. When you're in your deepest despair, as I was, remarkable things can happen. You'll see this in the chapters ahead.

The subjects in our examples all failed to gain control of their predicament through not applying conscious *awareness*. Their outcomes would have been happier had they had the knowledge and ability to avoid their suffering, despair, and misery before it overwhelmed them, possibly even ruined their lives entirely.

You can achieve this means of control only through learning Self-knowledge, through silencing your mind and rediscovering your Self-awareness, Self-realisation.

When you're Self-aware, that is to say, *aware of who you really are,* which is not your mind, your body or your ego, but something far greater, far more wonderful and omnipotent, and that your unwanted, unexpected thoughts and behaviour are nothing more than the results of your subconscious mind at work, then you can consciously step up and take back control of your thoughts and emotions.

Even real events, events that actually do happen to you, should not hinder your life or smother your happiness. All events are part of life, and to say we've had a life, we must experience them all, but we must also engage our conscious awareness to keep them all in perspective.

Think of conscious awareness, as the sixth gear in your gearbox. You can drive through life without ever engaging sixth gear (most people do), but it will always be at a higher cost, in terms of energy consumption. Engage sixth gear, and suddenly your engine's revolutions drop, life becomes less costly and the road ahead smoother, and your fuel load, your energy, is no longer so quickly depleted. You become more energy-efficient, more able to make long-journey decisions that will reach their full fruition.

Make it your life-journey-practice to learn to engage consciousness, conscious awareness. Engage sixth gear. Yes, you can!

I recommend that you make some brief notes here below, to remind yourself of events that you've experienced that, in hindsight and with your new knowledge, you can now clearly see were subconscious myths causing havoc.

....

....

....

....

....

....

....

....

....

....

....

....

....

....

....

....

Without awareness, our subconscious can be the source of great distress and our absolute undoing.

Think of conscious awareness as the sixth gear in your gearbox. You can drive through life without ever engaging sixth gear (most people do), but always at a higher cost in terms of energy consumption.

Engage sixth gear, and suddenly your engine's revolutions drop and life becomes less costly, the road ahead smoother, and your fuel load, your energy, is no longer so quickly depleted.

CHAPTER 9

Four Key Steps to Happiness

If you're suffering due to some emotional trauma, if you're experiencing intense or repeated bouts of unhappiness, misery, or despair and you wish it to end—and who doesn't?—the most important things you must do are also initially the most difficult.

The remedies you will need to employ to win back your happiness and personal power are explained in the last chapter. But before we get to that, here are the four key steps, four critical aspects, that you must first consciously *acknowledge* in order to achieve your goal.

1. Own the situation.

You must admit and concede that no other person brought it upon you.

Remembering the words of Maharishi, "Happiness [and unhappiness] is not due to external causes...." Blaming all and sundry on other persons will only deepen your darkness by generating further thoughts, perhaps thoughts of excusing yourself and shifting the responsibility for your pain and its purging to someone else, someone who may not even be aware that you're suffering. Equally detrimental to gaining relief is hiding yourself away from others, which will only bring isolation from possible help, prolonging your suffering.

2. Realise that your emotional state has arisen from your subconscious mind.

Consciously acknowledge this. Engaging conscious awareness will result in your realisation that your emotions and unhappiness are nothing more than a false or artificial emotional state; they're not real and can be overcome by silencing your subconscious.

Know that you are human, and as such it is a normal human condition you have fallen into. Know that your suffering is neither a permanent nor an insurmountable state. Consciously tell yourself that your preconditioned subconscious has always been a part of you, but that you are now aware of its existence and can counter its influence by silencing it with Self-awareness. Know that the painful emotions you're feeling are not real. Although they seem real, they're easy enough to dispel through your developing and exercising consciousness, Self-awareness.

When you've attained a state of Self-awareness, silencing your subconscious will be just like blowing away smoke!

3. Know that there is no other alternative but to develop Self-awareness.

If you are to overcome your unhappy condition (there are not several choices here, as with weight loss programs), seize the day and embrace the opportunity that your present suffering has presented to you. It is potentially the catalyst you've needed for your spiritual advancement and development. Use it as your vehicle to grow into a new level of consciousness, conscious Self-awareness, a *knowing* way of living.

Of course, to continue to allow your subconscious mind to influence your life, to remain unconscious, unrealised, and unknowing, means that you can expect to have to live with future bouts of unhappiness, perhaps throughout your life. Choosing to not act but to just hope that time will heal your pain will result in time indeed seeming to heal it, because eventually, as circumstances change, you will forget about it. But it will simply have retreated back into your subconscious mind. Where it will await your next crisis.

4. Don't put it off.

Be cognisant that remaining in ignorance or denial of your Self and responsibility for your life, and your happiness, leaves the door open for new unwanted issues to take up residence in your subconscious mind, to dwell there awaiting other crisis to arise in your life, to bring you further unhappiness and misery. You should repair the puncture before the tyre blows!

If your present dilemma doesn't move you to change, the next one will likely be a far more intense repetition or some new ugly surprise, possibly a serious financial or relationship disaster, an illness or drug or alcohol addiction, from which you cannot so easily extricate yourself. Unhappiness can lead to desperation, and desperation can lead to disaster. Know that until you learn to silence your mind and extinguish your uncontrolled thoughts the same kinds of unhappy experiences will be repeated time and time again, until you take conscious control and learn to extinguish that thing of darkness that causes them. And you'll constantly be living with the prospect of emotional discomfort. Know that you must learn now how to deal with your emotions, so that pain and unhappiness never return. Realise you must do it now!

In respect to this fourth key aspect, being great procrastinators means that we all have the propensity to put off this critical life-skill task, to put it off repeatedly, and so we return to our same painful old subconscious thought and behaviour patterns, and our consequent suffering. We're just innately slow to learn. By not reaching self-realisation, our subconscious, unrealised thinking will simply lead us back into the same old calamities again and again. That's the unhappy way an unrealised life is lived.

Learning how to overcome the uncontrolled thought processes is all empowering and will lead you to a higher position in life, to knowing, and to a life of enduring inner peace and happiness.

In writing these pages, I'm aware of my reiteration, of repeating certain key aspects. I'm just recapping the different possibilities within different readers' understandings of the subject. It wasn't my intention to confuse or to bore you. It was, however, my intention to deeply impress upon you the importance of those key aspects, because I want you to fully understand, fully grasp and comprehend, what is for some a tricky concept. Don't feel as if you've not got it, that it's beyond you. Trust me, it's not. As with understanding any subject that's new to you, another language perhaps, it's just a matter sometimes of repeated reading followed by quiet reflection and consideration. Followed by more repeated reading.

So please spend time on this, take it to heart, and reflect deeply upon it. It's an important subject. I'm hoping to have made the subject clearly and concisely comprehendible, to any reader. Are you having doubts about all this? Perhaps you're thinking; *I have had some disturbing thoughts at times, I have felt a bit fearful, suffered some emotional pain, but it was all due to someone else's bad behavior. Besides, I would never let my mind run away with me.*

Perhaps you're right. Time will tell. But if there's any kind of unhappiness in your life, you can be sure it's not real. It is perception, imagined. You can instantly overcome it by consciously stopping thinking.

Moving ahead, in order for you to reach your own proper and conclusive understanding about where your unhappiness comes from, and to have a true knowing about it, before we proceed further, I'm going to ask you to put this book down, to set a clock timer, and return to reading, in the next chapter, after a half hour has passed. That's when you're going to make the half hour following that available to perform what's called a *conscious recognition experience*. You're going to examine your emotional status, your unhappiness condition.

This is *not* a coffee break! I want you to come back relaxed, not wired. So please just go rest your mind for a while. Come back to this book in half an hour.

Know that your suffering is neither a permanent nor an insurmountable state.

Consciously tell yourself that your preconditioned subconscious has always been a part of you but that you are now aware of its existence and can counter its influence by silencing it with self-awareness.

Know that the painful emotions you're feeling are not real. Although they seem real, they're easy enough to dispel through your developing and exercising consciousness, Self-awareness

When you've attained Self-awareness, silencing your subconscious will be just like blowing away smoke!

Chapter 10

Conscious Recognition

Okay. Half an hour has passed? Are you ready now to face your demons? And, are you ready to embrace the prospect of enduring happiness?

To get the most effective result from this conscious recognition experience, you should undertake the exercise when you're able to fully recall and emotionally recreate your uncontrolled state of mind. Being emotionally back at the height of your pain and discomfort, in the depth of your despair, will generate the most authentic feelings and provide the opportunity to bring about the most effective end to it.

While that might sound difficult to achieve, for most people in the midst of an unhappy experience, it really isn't too difficult. You *can* do it by *consciously, mindfully recollecting, recreating* or *re-enacting* your unhappy emotional event. It is in fact integral to the success of the exercise and necessary for your successful accomplishment of reaching the state of Self- awareness.

The process is a simple one, that is to say, it's uncomplicated, but it's not easy, because you'll be doing this when your unhappiness and misery are at their worst, when those strong and upsetting emotions brought about by your focused, conscious thinking about the issue that upsets, deeply distresses, or angers you, arise fully in you, bringing you to a high level of emotional discomfort. So no, it's not easy. But it's *very* effective, and you *can* do it. Be brave. Be committed.

Remember that unhappy emotions arise to some degree in all of us, so although you may be sitting or standing there on your own, you're not alone in any other sense of the word. You are a part of all humankind. More importantly, critically, at this moment, you personally, are at the leading edge of human *self-realisation*.

The portal through which you will step into Self-awareness and consciousness is opening to you.

Now let's begin your journey to that place. To gain best effect in recreating the emotions that are causing your unhappiness, you are going to revisit your painful issue by mindfully *thinking about it in a totally focused way.* To do this, you must mentally revisit that event or person and the most recent circumstance that really upset you. It's a tough exercise, but remember, you *can* do it. And remember this, millions of people, myself included, have successfully undertaken this exercise and reaped the benefits. You can too.

Take some time now to relax and stay quiet while you concentrate. I recommend that you slowly read through this four-step exercise sequence a few times before you begin.

Here's how you'll do it.

Step 1

Find a quiet place, preferably alone, although if you are very emotionally upset, you may find it more effective to have someone you truly trust lead you through the process, and that's quite okay.

Sit quietly for a time, for some minutes, eyes closed. Many different thoughts will run through your mind.

When you've excluded all other thought subjects, precisely bring to mind (consciously think in a totally focused way) your particular anguishing event or the person concerned, and what happened, or what you did or what was done to you.

Recall as authentically and as accurately as you can, thinking hard about the detail. You must 'be there' again by using your mind to focus your thoughts hard on the subject for a good minute or two. See the event, the people, hear the voices.

Make it as real as possible.

As your mind recreates the event, you will quite naturally begin to feel the same emotions arise that arose in you when the event first happened. Unfortunately, this process can or will bring you some degree of emotional pain and discomfort, usually a knot in your solar plexus but possibly pressure in your head, followed by an increasing level of unhappy emotion, tears, perhaps anger or fear regret or jealousy, grief, or worry. If the event is something that really is affecting your life, you may begin to cry or become nervous and shaking. This is quite normal and is the state of emotion you need to achieve at this point in the exercise.

Allow the emotion to fill you. Hold that emotional state for a minute or longer if possible. Do not let anything distract you. Stay focused, let it envelop you, and, stay in it.

It's important to allow your emotions to rise fully and to really feel that emotion invade your body. Let it infiltrate your very being, let go any resistance to it and let it fill you.

Step 2

Having remained deep in your emotional state, reliving the recreated event, feeling fully your particular hurt, anger, jealousy, fear, grief or some phobia, whatever feelings and emotions have arisen for at least a couple of minutes, now, eyes still closed, bring yourself quickly into the present moment, and, using your conscious mind (the one you engage while reading this book), quite consciously and deliberately stop all thoughts about the unhappy event and instantaneously replace them with thoughts of something else. Make this new subject something pleasurable but completely unrelated to your former thoughts. (If you are undertaking the exercise alone, you may find it helpful to set a low volume alarm or bell to reawaken your consciousness after a predetermined time, say two minutes, to gently bring you back to the present moment, and to initiating your conscious happy thoughts.)

So you'll know exactly what subject you're going to switch to, predetermine this happy subject before you start your conscious recollection experience or process. If someone is helping you with this exercise, have that person well advised as to exactly what to tell you. Be sure to make it something that brings you happy feelings or, better still, feelings of utter joy. Make it the happiest moment in your life.

Step 3

Next, remaining in the present moment, using your intelligent conscious mind, consciously recognise (become consciously aware) that when you shifted your thoughts to the second, happy, subject that your former painful emotions instantly subsided, and the associated emotional pain stopped also.

Remarkable! So, how do you feel? Better? Lighter? Happier?

If you found a positive difference in your emotional state after your first time performing the exercise, congratulations! You have just instantly discovered that you *do* have control over your subconscious mind. More importantly, you have demonstrated to yourself—in the comfort and safety of your own home - that;

Your emotions are the result of, and directly connected to, your thoughts in the same moment.

See? No need for expensive professional help!

Only you can decide whether or not the performance of this initial exercise made an appreciable difference to your emotional state. Rest assured, however, that by your repeating the exercise, as many times as are necessary, you will eventually discover that you are not under the control of your mind. You will learn to understand your emotions, to manage your emotions, and to know how to avoid emotional pain whenever potentially unhappy or threatening events arise in your life. Because it's likely they *will* arise in your life in future, time and again. The difference in future however, will be your Self-awareness, your engaging conscious awareness, vigilance that stops the possibility of suffering, instantly. Forever, in future you will, as a matter of automatically applied consciousness, anticipate potential suffering and deal with it before it detrimentally impacts upon your life. You will live from a state of *knowing* not from thinking or believing.

Step 4

Now, *really* convince yourself of your true power over your mind by repeating that conscious recognition process over and over again. For best effect and a to attain a thorough understanding of the process, particularly when in the depths of unhappiness and struggling to overcome thoughts of your unhappy circumstances, you should initially practice several times a day. You can use it on different emotionally troubling issues and associated thoughts, and you can do this anywhere, anytime. You will soon eliminate all formerly disturbing thoughts and associated emotions from your being, replacing old, inhibiting mind-ful-ness with mind-less-ness, bliss, which happiness is.

You will quickly learn that you can control your life by controlling your emotions, by silencing and controlling your thoughts. Your subconscious will no longer have any say; will no longer dictate the terms of your life.

Now you are free to choose happiness at any time.

So, from today and for the rest of your life, each time and every time any emotionally disturbing thought pops into your head, consciously recognise it for what it is: Say to yourself; "*it's just a thought*". Immediately consciously shift your thoughts to some other, happier, subject and stay with that subject. Whistle a happy tune!

Feel your pain and suffering dissipate. Always keep your life in a happy place.

You can easily do this exercise while driving the car, walking on the beach, doing the dishes or any other activity, and of course, in any place you can find a quiet moment by yourself. I know I do.

Knowing that your thoughts are just thoughts and instantly recognising and acknowledging them as such *will totally empower you*. It will bring you not only peace in each and every moment you choose to experience it but also a whole new realistic and doable life paradigm, that mind/body state that is so often mysteriously referred to as Self-realisation that employs inner knowing, as opposed to external thinking or believing, *knowing* that it's your Self that controls your life, as opposed to your being constantly under the power and influence of your subconscious, your ego, your preconditioned mind.

Consider this notion for a moment: you can and do know what you know, but you can only believe what you believe or think. Knowing, in its purest form, is indisputable. Thoughts and beliefs, on the other hand, are something else altogether. Yes? Your beliefs are nothing more than concepts, repeated thinking, mind programming, or infusing ideas into your subconscious mind. Beliefs are simply ideas consolidated or fused into the mind. Nothing more. Hence, the existence the world's many religious and political beliefs, and so much distrust, divisiveness, and confusion. So many perceived gods. Come to know that your only true god, where unconditional love and guidance dwells, is within your Self.

It can be painful facing your demons during the conscious recognition experience, so you can be justifiably proud that you undertook the process and came out in one piece!

You'll agree now, that while it is not easy to reach realisation, it is a simple process. It just takes your being prepared to refresh your life paradigm and take a whole new course in life skills. The conscious recognition experience is certainly not rocket science and you *will* see and understand exactly how it works. And you can be sure it's not just another state of mind, another thought embedded in your subconscious. Your quick, *conscious* change of mind tricks your subconscious, exposing its workings and showing you how, if not understood and controlled by the conscious actions of the Self, when left to its own devices, your powerful mind can initiate that whole range of archived emotions within your subconscious, keeping you stuck in them and held there under its control, under the influence of its preconditioning, its processes, and in a state of whatever it decides. That is, until the conscious Self steps in and takes back control, putting the mind back in its box! All this good comes from *Self*-awareness.

The exercise you undertook effectively got you outside of and beyond the influence of the subconscious mind. Beyond its ability to control your outer-self, which control would otherwise block you from your connection to your inner Self. Like switching a radio receiver from one station or frequency band, to another, conscious recognition re-awakens and empowers a deeper force within you, your true Self, your inner Self, stimulating it to resume its true position ... that of the boss, totally in charge in every situation.

From now on, though, you are your own therapist. And you can help others to understand their emotions too, by showing *them* how to perform the conscious recognition exercise. You have just truly empowered yourself, so you *can* also empower others who may be suffering unhappiness through emotional pain, your children, your spouse, your best friend. Loan them this book, or buy them their own copy.

The best present you could ever give someone is the key to their Self-empowerment, and their enduring happiness.

Make some notes here about your perceived unhappy experiences and how by using conscious recognition, you quickly gained control of them. Which ones seemed more stubborn? How did you persist and overcome them, dissolving them back into nothing?

....

....

....

....

....

....

....

....

....

....

....

....

....

....

....

....

....

It's important to allow your emotions to rise fully and really feel that emotion invade your body. Let it infiltrate your very being, let go any resistance to it and let it fill you.

Your emotions are the result of and directly connected to your thoughts in the same moment.

You will quickly learn to control your life by controlling your emotions by controlling your thoughts. Your subconscious will no longer have any say, will no longer dictate the terms of your life.

Now you are free to choose happiness at any time.

CHAPTER 11

Intuition

For absolute clarity about this thing we've called the *Self*, let's approach it from another angle. Have you heard of, talked about, or experienced what's known as intuition? Few people ever take this subject seriously, but they should, because *intuition* is another way to describe the workings of our inner *Self*. It is the manifestation of our *Self's* knowing.

The Self is sometimes called soul or spirit. It's the pure consciousness aspect of you that communicates with your outer self (your mind, body, or ego) through its silent voice, through its' knowing. It is pure unhindered conscious intelligence, the place from where all knowing is available to you. It's your one reliable source for guidance, for effecting your life decisions and direction.(unlike your subconscious). You need only acknowledge it, listen to it and heed it. But first and foremost, you must become aware of it. Become Self-aware.

Too often we totally disregard our intuition, confusing it with other thoughts and often to our detriment. Does "Oh, why didn't I listen to myself'?" sound familiar? When you last experienced such an event, you knew that that feeling was strong, nagging at you, and actually made you consider taking a certain action. But before you could act, your subconscious mind jumped in, and you mindfully thought, "I'm being silly. I think I'll do something else." You ignored your silent intuition, your inner Self, which was a big mistake. Because your subconscious, directing you from its archived information, your old past experiences, was in no position to give you instructions about a new experience. However, remember *Felix culpa*? The fortunate error or lucky mistake? Use these experiences to your advantage, for your opportunity to awaken to conscious awareness.

Going back briefly to our examples in chapter 8 – example 4 - the young student must have intuitively felt terribly guilty when she opened those computer files. Intuitively, she surely knew it was the wrong thing to do and that there would surely be repercussions. But her subconscious preconditioning of fear of loss gave rise to her fear and suspicion and made her dig deeper into her imagination as it drew on past experiences. Then, as if to reinforce its decision, to prove it-self right, it concocted a further convoluted story about the boyfriend's unfaithfulness. It did this so cleverly and convincingly that she brought the whole event into reality, but it was only ever *her* reality.

Likewise, in our example of Bob and his litany of accusation and abuse, his intuition, his inner feelings should have set alarm bells ringing. Perhaps they did, but his subconscious mind was just too powerful, too convincing and influential.

Living life purely as your minds host, being the vessel in which it lives, its' container or the vehicle it gets around in, somewhere for it to be – lodged securely inside an unconscious being – will afford your subconscious mind the chance to dictate the terms of your life, always making you go where it thinks you should go, making you do what it thinks you should do.

Your awakening to conscious awareness will dislodge it, bringing about its redundancy!

You can see how people have inadvertently but effectively handed the controls over to their subconscious, making it their compass for direction, an encyclopaedia or source of all knowledge, that place they always go to and depend upon, both for advice and to act from. You and I and everyone else we know have had the same apprenticeship. We're all taught the same stuff, in the same way. The same unconscious, mind-full way. And life just didn't work out the way we expected, nor did it deliver us the happiness we hoped for.

Instead of misinformation providing you with misdirection, in future you'll want your life to be headed in a better direction. Obviously, that can happen only if you live life from a completely different reference point, from knowing, and by using your mind consciously, as a tool, a source of usefulness in your life, thereby not allowing it to become the source of painfulness in your life.

What do you think about that? Be careful now ... it's a trick question. And now that you're Self aware, you can no longer be tricked.

Importantly, you can simply give up the need to think about it entirely. Because, from today on, you will *know*, and therein will lay your peace, your contentment with whatever is. Pure happiness.

After all, it's not your problem, is it? Thinking about it will only cause your subconscious to scour its archives, searching for more old, wrong answers, more thoughts and solutions to trick you into believing something and then you'll have to start the whole process over again.

I imagined you just said, "Aha, yes, that all makes sense. My view is crystal clear. But what, if anything, should I do now?"

So I'm saying back to you; "Good. By that statement it's clear that you've understood what *not* to do. And that's one giant leap forward."

But to answer your question, in the next and last chapter, you'll learn what next to do. It's the simplest part of your quest for happiness, but perhaps initially the hardest part. You must next consciously apply patience and perseverance if you are to reach that elusive state of being, enduring happiness.

You must learn to be *still*. Learn to be *nothing*.

The self is sometimes called soul or spirit. It communicates with your outer self (your mind, body, or ego) through its silent voice, through its knowing. It is conscious intelligence, the place from where all knowing is available to you. It's a reliable source, unlike your subconscious. You need only to acknowledge it, listen to it and heed it before acting. But first and foremost, you must be aware of it.

Living life purely as your mind's host, being the vessel in which it lives, its container or the vehicle it gets around in, somewhere for it to be - lodged securely inside an unconscious being - will afford your subconscious mind the chance to dictate the terms of your life, always making you go where it thinks you should go, making you do what it thinks you should do.

Importantly, you can simply give up the need to think about it entirely. Because you will know, and therein will lay your peace, your contentment with whatever is. Enduring happiness.

CHAPTER 12

Enduring Happiness

"Finally," I hear you sigh.

Following your reading my hopefully enlightening preamble, the lengthy dialogue of new ideas, revelations, anecdotes and confessions woven throughout the eleven preceding chapters, you are, I hope, better prepared for enduring happiness. You are ready now to move forward with un-blinkered eyes, with a much wider, much deeper field of view. This is the true view, which can be seen only when the mind is no longer the lens.

Your only remaining challenge towards reaching the ultimate goal of all humanity, Self-realisation—that state of being from where, with absolute clarity of mind, you will not fail to bring about enduring happiness in your life—is to do nothing.

Engage your conscious awareness, and consider this statement:

Clarity of mind=clear of your mind = mind-less-ness =no mind.

Happily, you won't have to climb a stony, misty trail to some mountaintop, to sit, hungry and cross-legged for years, in order to reach this state of being. You know now that that's just another popular belief!

Knowing now that your mind is not you but is the mechanism or tool your Self uses consciously, to imagine or to figure things out, it's imperative and the essence of your revealing truth and reality in your life, that you learn to accomplish and effect automatic, instinctive control over it at all times and in any given situation.

This accomplishment and practice will be an integral function in your life from today and forever. It will become the very foundation of all that you are, underpinning your every action and putting real meaning and enduring happiness back in your life.

In your next and most profound step to enduring happiness, you will learn to completely stop your thoughts, at any time of the day or night, by simply being still.

Stilling or silencing your mind will put you directly in touch with your all-knowing inner Self.

Here's where some people get further confused and start thinking, "Oh. Okay. Now I know what he's talking about, I'll meditate." Please ... no! Stop right there!

This subject has been widely misunderstood, the very word *meditation* conveys many different ideas to many people. For example, universally, meditation is most often understood to be an act of sitting and thinking about a subject in a focused way. So, please, if that's your understanding of meditation, do not meditate. Do not *think* of anything. If, on the other hand, your understanding of meditation is to silence the mind, then, praise-be, you've got it right.

Silent meditation is what is required.

To simply be quiet, to be still, think of nothing. That is to say, don't think at all.

Thinking requires you to engage the mind, which requires you to make some effort. Make no effort. Do nothing. Think nothing. Be nothing. Realize that you are nothing. No thing. Silently, find no-thing-ness.

It's a simple, one-step process this time. Are you ready to do this?

The One Step to Nothing

Go to your quiet place, sit quietly and comfortably, close your eyes. Be still. That is to say, every time a thought crops up (it's likely many will) shift your mind away from each and any thought. Importantly, not to some other thought this time, but simply, quietly, let it just drift on past until you're in the open space between any thoughts, in ... nothing. Find nothingness.

Stay there. In time no-thing-ness will become stillness.

In stillness you will eventually experience silence.

Allow yourself to be immersed in silence.

Stay there but remain conscious, conscious only of your breathing.

Wait.......wait to see what comes in the silence, from nothingness, and from no-thing-ness and stillness.

What is that that is there in the silence?

Know this. You will very likely not reach no-thing-ness on your first try. That's because you'll be trying. But do not be disillusioned. No-thing-ness only ever arrives when you you're *not* trying. Each time you undertake this process, which may take several minutes or longer, above all else, practise patience. Initially, perhaps hours of patience. Perhaps days of patience. It doesn't matter. It will be patience well spent. It's imperative that you simply sit quietly to reach stillness. Remember to not *try* to reach it. It will not come if you try. When you do reach it, you will know. It's a knowing that will be with you forever. Silencing your ever-busy mind will bring you incredible clarity of mind. You will never again fall under the control of your subconscious.

It's highly likely you haven't taken any notice of your *Self* for a very long time, so your *Self* may not respond immediately. You need to silently reintroduce yourself to your Self. In time, through patient practice, in stillness, Self reveals itself.

It's been wisely said that you can't discover Self; you can only uncover it. Because, like your happiness, it's always been there, waiting for you. Contemporaneous with your *awareness* of the presence of Self, you may feel a lightness of mind, an inner calm, and quite unexpectedly, an uplifting inner happiness. You'll realise that you're smiling. And not because you *thought* you won the lotto!

Realising Self is a far more profound experience.

It's an everlasting experience.

Happily, you won't have to climb a stony, misty trail to some mountaintop, to sit, hungry and cross-legged for years, in order to reach this state of being. You know now that that's just another popular belief!

In your next and most profound step to enduring happiness, you will learn to completely stop your thoughts, at any time of the day or night, by simply being still.

Silent meditation is what is required.

To simply be quiet, to be still, think of nothing. That is to say, don't think at all.

CHAPTER 13

Living From Your New Reality

Chapter 13? They say thirteen is lucky for some! But knowing now that your understanding and applying The Happiness Secret in your life is not due to luck or auspicious timing, nor to anyone else's directing you. It's solely due to you engaging your own conscious intelligence so that you will no longer be tricked by your subconscious, by others or by superstition. Right?

Here's the really interesting part. As you go about life having reached this ultimate state, Self-awareness, you'll begin to see other people's behaviour for what it really is, and see it without any need for judgment. You'll *know* that theirs is not bad behaviour, just unconscious, unrealised, unenlightened behaviour. You'll have no difficulty making allowances and adjustments for them, ducking out of the way of what you used to consider alarming or confronting events, like people shouting, being aggressive, stubborn, demanding, unbending, and generally ill at ease with the world. And you'll smile inwardly, not conceitedly, but knowingly. And, most interestingly, you'll see it coming whenever it begins to arise again in your own behaviour! Because, at times it will. You'll see others—and yourself—being tricked by subconscious thoughts. You'll remember mild paranoia, when the subconscious mind generates thoughts of suspicion of others that when associated with emotional pressure, become false or invented beliefs. False beliefs that, in one's mind-full-ness, are parallel to, but not actually truths, facts, or reality. You *know* what I mean.

In future, with clarity of mind through self-awareness, you'll see all the people of the whole wide world and all life's events for what they really are. Not what your old subconscious would like you to believe they are. What a relief!

Most of us have at one stressful time or another, to one degree or another, suffered the unhappiness condition. Many suffer all their lives. Practising silencing the mind and engaging Self-awareness, will help you to see mind-full-ness coming towards you, and you'll be able to take early action to avoid it. You'll *know* to take into account the fact that you and other people are not seeing the world for what it really is, that your expressed views are distorted by your conditioned mind, by mindfulness, distorted through the blurred lens of your subconscious.

Thoughts of certain past events or people may spring to mind as you read this, but don't let them. Instead, consciously stop any thoughts about them now; and stop any emotional attachment to any thought. Because you can now see that thinking about past events from a intellectually conscious point of view, are a demonstration of your ability to use your conscious intelligent mind usefully. To use it to create an image or a hypothetical example of an event, where you (or some other person) in your former state of unconscious unawareness, allowed the preconditioned subconscious to misguide and control them, all the way to unhappiness.

Now you can see why each persons' "truth" is so different. When viewed through the subconscious mind, which has been programmed by each individuals' lifetime experiences where events and emotions are recorded and archived. These are recreated in the mind and in action, quite often inappropriately, when the subconscious is triggered by some current event. Each person's subconscious taught them to *believe,* taught them that certain matters are affected in a certain way, taught them to behave and react in certain ways and to expect certain outcomes from various events and circumstances. These *beliefs* have thereby become each individuals 'truths'.

The simple fact is that people simply become disappointed, disillusioned, disenchanted, perhaps angry and ultimately unhappy, when those truths did not work out for them, when their *expectations* were not met. It's perhaps like a toddler who throws a tantrum over an insignificant event, and who's already learned in his very short life to expect a certain outcome from his actions; Cry, and mum comes running; Cry louder, and mother brings food and comfort. i.e. I get attention when I cry.

Cry all night, and the woman stays with me all night! Yes!

Without conscious awareness, without self-realisation, when the boy or girl becomes a man or woman, he or she will likely still expect his or her 'crying' to be met with soothing sex or gourmet food. Some expect money, most expect exclusive attention and the reduction of their pain.

"Make my pain go away, or I'll cry louder." – or - Pay up or I'll divorce you, leave you, sue you, assault you and steal from you! All these are common threats from unconsciously, unaware people who are effectively saying;

"Everything I do for you is conditional upon the outcome I'm going to get in return."

"I know this is to be true because I learned it at a very early age—it stuck in my subconscious mind, where it remains."

"I never learned any different."

Such a man acting in this way in a later stage in life, perhaps at forty-something, discovering himself out of work, married with children and with a mortgage, would possibly receive a quite different response from the new woman in his life whose reply might be; "Well, sweetie! It's time for you to learn another way. The way of emotional pain. You see dear, I'm leaving you, because you're not giving me the outcomes *I* expected!"

In other words, "Get lost, you moron, I'm suing you for half the house!"

Unfortunately, family courts and the people who compose, create, and implement our laws and legislation have not themselves' yet attained a state of Self-awareness, Self-realization. Nor have most people we encounter on this planet, so the outcomes we get from those people and from our justice systems often seem like injustice.

All our truths would all be the same if only we were all more *Self-aware.*

We are after all, one people and all capable of truly understanding one another through applying conscious Self-awareness, and mind-less-ness in respect to dealing with life's challenging experiences. If only we would make it a priority as a nation to make it part of our children's early education, and as individuals to make the time ourselves to learn to attain a state of conscious awareness. Then, when dealing with our lives' achievements and challenges it would be as fundamental as breathing to bring about peace in the world, and happiness as a way of life for all. Bring it on!

The information I've imparted in this book has been my offering to you dear reader, to help you create a happier life. It's knowledge about what conscious intellectual thinking is; a program for not thinking too much. I'm certain that the intellectually, consciously performed exercises offered for you to practise at home, *will* enhance your own life's journey. My hope is that you will have gleaned from this book, some useful new ideas and concepts for building enduring happiness into your own life. It's my own small offering of wisdom, derived from my own self-awareness, derived from my own not-so-happy life experiences.

Beautifully summarizing the essence of the concepts herein, and something for us all to reflect upon; these most profoundly definitive points of view so wisely conveyed by the widely respected twenty-first-century spiritualist and philosopher, and my favourite guru, Thomas Moore, in his wonderful books about the *Soul*. Moore's view is; it matters not that we label some of life's experiences good, and some bad, what matters is that we learn to embrace them all, growing through them knowing that they're all nutritious!

So dear reader, be vigilant, and remember Thomas Moore's truth about the nutrition in each life experience as you navigate your future route and redesign your old life paradigm. You'll know from now on to be careful about what you include, and from what place you think. Remember to create milestones, those waypoints on your track ahead, so that whenever it arises, you'll arrest the noise and babble within your mind. Recognise that it's most likely irrelevant to the truth and to your best interests. Look inwardly for advice and listen to your heart, which is your true Self, as you take stock of how well your life's journey is proceeding. Make any necessary changes along the way, consciously, to keep your heading true, as you're doing now. Demonstrate to your conscious Self that you know the way and that you won't ever again allow your subconscious mind control of the wheel.

Go ahead now and find your own enduring happiness, and spread it around. It's free and so will you be, for the rest of your life. Free from out-of-control thinking. Free from any need to know. It's a great feeling, isn't it? Always be smiling ... that inner smile!

Consider this not ...

The End

... but your New Beginning.

Author's Hope

My hope for you is that reading about *my* life experience and my discovering self will have brought new awareness into your own life. Through following the teachings within this little book of wisdom, you *can* choose a happier route through life. I hope that in the future you'll know to be careful about what you think! And that you will never again allow your subconscious mind control of your life.

Remember that enduring happiness is your natural state of being. It's your right to achieve and retain, throughout your life. To uncover your inner happiness, discover your inner Self!

Please remember that in order to have happiness on tap and available to you at any time of the day or night, it's critical to make time every day to be still, to listen to, and to feel the connection to your self, to your knowing. Practise silencing your mind and happiness *will* become your natural state of being.

I highly recommend that you begin this new way of being by attending an authentic silent retreat, to remain in silence for five to seven days. And let silence work its wonders.

May your whole life be lived in.....

Enduring Happiness.

Be still, and see what comes.

Know that your true god is your Self.

In stillness, Self is revealed.

*Revealing Self will reward you
with enduring happiness.*

About the Author

Born in New Zealand in 1949, Stephen moved to Australia in 1985 in search of a fresh start after a series of personal life calamities. Not until ten further unhappy years elapsed and a 'final straw' disaster struck, did his awakening to truth unfold. But ultimately, it was through dealing with the fallout of a devastating personal relationship event, that lead him to the discovery of 'The Happiness Secret', the secret to enduring happiness. Using understandable language, he brings together the wisdom of the Gurus of spiritual awakening and the capacity that ordinary people possess to understand it by offering so much more than chicken soup comfort in his true and very personal account of life experience and Self-discovery. His book is an effective learning instrument and perhaps the catalyst you needed, to create your own better, happier life.

Stephen shows how seemingly insurmountable, emotionally challenging events can be hugely diminished, even instantly disintegrated, into nothing more than they really are; uncontrolled thoughts. His work displays a clear understanding about the most prevalent, detrimental human condition of all, the suffering of unhappiness, and it will open the door to happiness for millions, a door they never knew existed, nor possibly would ever have dared to open without such sincere, down to earth guidance.

After re-discovering his inner happiness, Stephen has also re-discovered his ideal living environment, in peaceful surroundings by the beach again. Together with his wife, June, Stephen enjoys life, traveling, writing, and sailing boats. As he says; "Ours' is now a life of enduring happiness acquired through *Self*-awareness and by applying conscious intelligence, vigilance, to all of our life decisions. That's what gives us a sharper view of the world from a calmer and happier perspective."

"Living life 'in the dark', in an *unconscious* state ruled by the subconscious mind, is like having to shop for your favourite food in a foreign supermarket. Nothing offered on the shelves ever seems quite what you want, but, because you can't read the labels, you never really know why. Conversely, like a home cooked meal, life's all the tastier when you've imagined it, selected the ingredients, and baked it yourself. Then you *know; Ah, yes,* that's how my meals should taste"

"Isn't that how you want *your* life to be?".

Recommended Reading

I highly recommend the following works which will enhance and complement your understanding of the subject of this book.

Your Erroneous Zones Dr Wayne Dyer
1997 2009 Piatkus Books

You Are That - I & II Gangaji 1995 Gangaji Foundation

Soul Mates Thomas Moore 1994 Harper Collins

Absolute Happiness Michael Rowlands
1993 Self Communications

Silence Your Mind Dr Ramesh Manocha 2013 Hachette Aus